still
HERE

True stories of the moments
that changed everything

MATT GILHOOLY

For Joan, Jack, and Eva.
You are the reason I started listening.

And for everyone who has heard me say "*did you listen to The Life Shift this week?*" more times than they can count – thank you for putting up with me. This one's for you, too.

TABLE OF CONTENTS

SECTION 2: WHEN THE MOMENT WAS QUIET

SECTION 3: WHAT THE BODY KNOWS

SECTION 6: WHEN LOVE IS THE REASON

Jaclyn L. – The Night Her Sister's House Felt Different
Claudia N. – She Moved Her Car First
Susan L. – My Brother Shouldn't Be Home on a Thursday
Laurel W. – Daddy's Girl
Cyra D. – The Choice She Made When She Was Sixteen
Matt F. – Brokedown Palace
Jackie F. – The Morning She Left for the Hospital
Brianna L. – All This Love and Nowhere to Put It
Kristina A. – The Stranger's Question
Barb H. – Her Legs Were Completely Still
Nadia C. – I'm Done
Rebe H. – The Plane Home From Cuba
Mathilde F. – I Need to Live This Life for Him
Tanmeet S. – Why Not Us?
Sally M. – Four of Them Got in a Canoe
Kathleen Q. – The Recliners
Lori K. – I Brought Him Here

SECTION 7: THE DOOR YOU DIDN'T KNOW WAS THERE

SECTION 8: THE SECRET YOU CARRIED

Still Listening

THE LINE THAT STARTED EVERYTHING

I was eight years old when my father's boss's wife picked me up from day camp. That was the first sign something was wrong.

It was a small thing – someone I barely knew, someone who had no reason to be there – but I felt it immediately, in my stomach, before my brain had caught up. We drove to my father's office. He sat me down. And he told me that my mother had been killed in a motorcycle accident.

That sentence is my line in the sand. Everything before it is one life. Everything after it is another.

I didn't know that at the time. I was eight. I just knew that the world had changed shape and I had to figure out how to live in the new one. Which I did, mostly by pretending the old one hadn't existed. For a long time, I thought that was coping. I understand now that it was just postponing.

Decades later, in my thirties, a therapist said something to me that I've thought about almost every day since: every decision you've made since your mother died has been made by that scared eight-year-old. I had never considered that. I had never considered that the child who absorbed all that grief and tucked it away and got very good at seeming fine had been running the show the whole time, making choices from a place of fear I wasn't even aware of.

That sentence changed me. It sent me back to grieve properly, finally, and it also sent me toward something I hadn't expected: **curiosity**.

I started wondering whether other people had moments like mine. A single sentence, a phone call, a parking lot – something that split their lives into before and after. I suspected they did. I didn't know how many, and I didn't know what shape those moments would take.

I started a podcast to find out. I called it The Life Shift. I sat across from strangers – over two hundred and fifty of them now, from around the world – and I asked them about their line in the sand. What was the moment? What did it feel like? What did your life look like on the other side of it?

What I found surprised me. Some of the moments were devastating – the phone calls, the diagnoses, the losses that redrew everything. But some of them were quiet. Some were beautiful. A door appearing where there wasn't one before. A decision that finally felt true. A sentence that gave a name to something good that had been growing without a name. The line in the sand doesn't only mark loss. Sometimes it marks arrival.

This book is what I found.

I want to be clear about what this book is and isn't. It isn't a collection of inspirational stories, though many of them are inspiring. It isn't a grief manual or a self-help guide, though I believe you will find yourself in these pages. It isn't a companion to the podcast, though every person here has an episode you can find and listen to.

This is a book of moments. Just the instant itself – the thing that happened, described as precisely and honestly as I can, with no backstory and no resolution. And then, after each one, a few lines from me: the listener. Not analysis. Not advice. Just what I heard, and what I think it might mean for you.

I have been changed by every single conversation in here. Not because the stories are dramatic – some of them are, some of them are quiet, some of them are full of joy – but because each one reminded me of something I keep forgetting: that every person you pass on the street has a line in the sand. A moment when everything split. A version of themselves they carry quietly, alongside the version they show the world.

This book is an invitation to stop for a moment and pay attention to that. To yours, and to everyone else's.

My line was September 1, 1989. You'll find it in Section 2, alongside the others whose moments arrived quietly, the way mine did. But my line is really just the reason I started listening.

What I found when I did is the rest of this book.

section 1

THE GROUND GIVES WAY

Some moments don't ask permission.
They don't build slowly or send signals.
They just arrive –
a phone call, a parking lot,
a door opening at the wrong time –
and when they do, the version of you that existed
ten seconds ago is already gone.

You don't know that yet.
That's the thing about the ground giving way.
You don't feel it until you're already falling.

I've sat with a lot of people
who lived through the moments in this section.
What I noticed, every time, is that they found a way
to put the next foot forward.
Not immediately. Not gracefully. But eventually.
The ground gave way, and they were still there
when it stopped.

MINDY C.

Something Good Has to Come From This

On a Palm Sunday in April 2014, Mindy's younger son had a lacrosse game – but it was rained out, so she headed instead to pick up her older son from a singing audition he was at with her father. She arrived in the parking lot minutes after a white supremacist gunman had murdered them both. She didn't know yet. She just saw the truck, the open doors, her father's body. Then she felt something push her shoulders back, heard words she couldn't explain, and walked around the truck to find two strangers already holding her son.

FOR YOU

Most of us will never be tested the way Mindy was.
But the impulse she followed that night –
to reach outward, to speak at the vigil, to mean every word –
is not something you plan.

It lives in you already.

You don't have to know what you'll do in the worst moment.
You just have to trust that something in you will know.

MINDY C.

**Something Good Has to
Come From This**

SYLVIA M.

Her Son's Bat

Eight months after her son was murdered at nineteen, Sylvia pulled into her garage and opened her car door. A man stepped into that space. She knew immediately – the question about directions was a pretense. She said sure, let me get out and show you, and when she did she ran. He grabbed her by the hair. They fought all the way to his car. She ended up in the back seat, saw his license plate, grabbed her son's baseball bat, screamed the number until he drove away. The DA told her later he had told police he was just trying to kill someone. She was his fourth victim. She was the only one who got his plate.

FOR YOU

For eight months after her son died,
Sylvia said she hadn't cared whether she lived or not.

Then someone tried to take that choice from her,
and something in her fought back anyway.

That something lives in all of us.
You may not know it's there until you need it.

But it's there.

SYLVIA M.

Her Son's Bat

MICHELLE H.

Turn Around and Walk Back to Your Car

She was driving home when she already knew. She had spent thirty years at America's Most Wanted, arriving at crime scenes before families did, standing on the other side of the police tape. Now she was pulling up to the first home she had shared with her husband – where he carried her over the threshold, where they brought her daughter home – and there were police lights and ambulances and police tape. Her pastor was standing there. He grabbed her out of the car, held her, and said two words: it's true. Her daughter was seven years old.

FOR YOU

The things we spend our lives preparing for
are never the things that find us.

Michelle had stood at a hundred crime scenes.
None of it prepared her for her own.

What carried her through wasn't preparation.
It was the decision, made very early and held onto hard,
that her daughter's story would be about who she was in the
world – not what happened to her.

That decision is available to all of us,
in whatever loss we're living with.

MICHELLE H.

Turn Around and
Walk Back to Your Car

STEPHEN P.

I'm Sorry, But I Just Pronounced Your Son Dead

They were twelve minutes into the drive to Rhode Island, flying down I-95, when the phone rang again and connected through the car speaker. His younger son was eleven years old and leaning forward between the two front seats. A doctor introduced himself, paused, and said: I'm sorry, but I just pronounced your son dead. Everything went black. Stephen had no business driving but somehow found the right lane, took the first exit, ran a light, and came to a screeching stop in an empty bank parking lot on a Sunday afternoon. They opened the doors and started screaming at the sky, running in circles until they collided and fell to the ground. The doctor was still on the phone. His wife was clutching it in one hand.

FOR YOU

There is no right way to receive the worst news.

Running in circles in a bank parking lot on a Sunday afternoon
is a right way.

Screaming at the sky is a right way.

Clutching the phone of the person who just told you is a right
way.

The body does what it has to do
to hold something that shouldn't fit inside a person.

You don't have to be dignified in the moment that breaks you.

You just have to get off the highway.

STEPHEN P.

I'm Sorry, But I Just Pronounced
Your Son Dead

JENN D.

I Can Feel My Fingers and Toes

She was driving home, watching the reservoir out the window and wondering if it had frozen over yet, when her eyes snapped back to the road and there was a semi truck too close. She tried to get around it. The second trailer caught the front passenger side of her car. It went end over end three times, then sideways, until it came to rest and she was hanging upside down. A man peeled back the windshield. She looked at his face and knew from his expression that she was not okay. She was too afraid to look at her own body, so she closed her eyes and wiggled her fingers and toes. She could feel them. She took an Uber home that same day, walked in the front door, heard kids screaming and saw pizza on the counter and someone going by on rollerblades – and stood there sobbing because she had almost never gotten to be part of this anymore. Then a few weeks later the police called to say they had rebuilt the accident every way they could and there was no survivable scenario.

FOR YOU

Jenn learned something hanging upside down in that car
that she carried up every mountain after it:
close your eyes, wiggle your fingers and toes,
feel what is actually true.

Everything else is a story you're writing.

You can stop that story and start a different one.

The moment she understood that we don't get to choose
when we leave
but we do get to choose how we live –
that understanding is available to all of us.

We just usually need something to shake it loose.

JENN D.

I Can Feel
My Fingers and Toes

LAURA L.

It Hurts Everywhere, Mama

Cecilia was almost four and something wasn't right. Laura had taken her to the doctor more than once. Nothing, they said. One night she was in bed with her daughter, tickling her before sleep, and she asked: tell me where it hurts, baby. Cecilia rubbed her hands all over her entire body and said: everywhere, mama. Laura went cold. She knew. She insisted on a blood draw. Her daughter had cancer.

FOR YOU

Laura said she had a feisty side she had been tamping down a
little.

That night in the dark,
with her daughter's hands moving over her own body,
the feisty side came back and didn't leave.

Most of us have something like that inside us –
a fierce knowing,
a protective instinct,
a voice that says: *no. This is not okay. I have to fight.*

You don't have to wait for a crisis to start listening to it.

But if a crisis is what it takes, that voice will be there.
Laura's was.

LAURA D.

It Hurts Everywhere, Mama

TARRIS M.

It's Happening

She had a dream career in fashion – fifteen years as a buyer, a merchandise planner, someone who had sketched fashion since she was a girl and then actually built the life she had imagined. A doctor had told her something about her eyes, about a hereditary condition called Stargardt's disease, and had said it wouldn't progress. One morning she woke up, reached for her phone, and started scrolling. She couldn't see. She lay there and said to herself: it's happening. The one thing he said wouldn't happen is happening. Her career in fashion required her to see. She could no longer see the way she needed to. Everything she had built toward was gone.

FOR YOU

Tarris said she had always been someone who could take a
hard thing and find a way to grow from it,
even as a child.

That capacity didn't make the morning easier.

It just meant she had something to work with when the
morning came.

Whatever has been taken from you that you
spent years building –
the grief of it is real.

The question of what to build next can wait.

First, you have to let the morning be what it is.

TARRIS M.

It's Happening

ROBYN D.

The Whiteboard

She was 29 years old and alone in the hospital room – COVID protocols meant one visitor for four hours a day, and the hours were up. Her arm had turned completely purple from her fingertips to her shoulder the night before. That morning her surgeon walked in, and no one had explained anything yet. Good news, he said, what you have is most likely fixable. Bad news, it's going to be a very long journey. He wrote it on the whiteboard: a week in the hospital, surgery, then a month later her first rib removed, then another surgery after that. She said it felt like watching a movie of her own life. She looked at his face to understand what her face was doing.

FOR YOU

Robyn had spent years going, going, going –
filling every hour, never sitting still, always moving.

The thing that finally made her stop was not a choice.

It was a purple arm and a whiteboard
and a surgeon who handed her a tissue.

Sometimes, the life we actually want
is on the other side of the full stop we
would never have chosen.

That's not a comforting thought.

But it's a true one.

ROBYN D.

The Whiteboard

SUNNY C.

The Trail of Blood

His mother had attempted suicide once before, when he was fourteen – she left a note, left her phone, drove to a parking garage. She was found before she jumped. She got help. She got better. She drove him to school, came to his games, had a boyfriend, had a cousin and two young daughters move in with her. Things were good. And then Sunny went to college, and the empty nest hit her hard, and in June of 2016, he got a call from his dad. She had gone back to the same parking garage. She had jumped from the second floor. The only reason she was found was that someone followed a trail of blood.

FOR YOU

Sunny was eighteen or nineteen.
He said he still didn't fully understand what mental health was.

The guilt and the regret came in hard –
all the questions of what he could have done differently.

He said a manager at Google later told him
he had survived a suicide attempt
and the one thing he most wanted his kids to know
was that there was nothing they could have done.

You can't be the person who holds someone together by
proximity.
You can love them in the way you are capable of loving
at the age you are.

That is enough.

It has to be.

SUNNY C.

The Trail of Blood

ROBERT P.

My Parents Weren't There

His brother complained of a stomachache that morning. Robert thought he was faking it – he knew all the tricks, had hidden in basements and closets himself to avoid school. His parents finally relented and took his brother to the doctor. Robert went to school. He mostly forgot about it. He might have been a little jealous that his brother got to stay home. And then the school day ended, and he walked out, and his parents weren't there to pick him up.

FOR YOU

Robert didn't know yet what the empty pickup line meant.

He just knew it was wrong.

Sometimes the first sign is that simple –
the person who is always there, isn't.

Before you know, you know.

That moment of wrongness before the words arrive
is the body registering the truth.

Whatever you have felt in a moment like that was real.

The knowing came before the telling.

ROBERT P.

My Parents Weren't There

CHRISTELLE B.

You Are Going Back to Cameroon

She had known since she was young that if she was ever going to leave Cameroon, it would be to go to the United States. When the opportunity came she applied for her visa, boarded a plane, and landed at LAX. An immigration officer detained her. He was a large man – he said he had to lean across the table to get to eye level with her because she was tall. He looked her in the eyes and said: *you know what I think? I think you came here to work as a prostitute. So you are going back to Cameroon.* She had done nothing wrong. The accusation was baseless. The legal battle to clear her name would be long. She had just arrived at the place she had been building toward her whole life, and the first thing it said to her was no.

FOR YOU

Christelle had always been the strong one –
the person other people leaned on.

The system that was supposed to be a gateway
told her she didn't belong
before she had taken a single step through it.

What happened next was a legal fight
and an advocacy career
and a life built anyway.

Sometimes the door that was supposed to open
is the one that tests whether you were serious
about walking through it.

She was serious.

CHRISTELLE B.

You Are Going Back to Cameroon

DANIEL R.

The Mono That Wasn't Mono

He was seven years old. His older brother was ten. His brother wasn't feeling well, and then they took him to the doctor, and the doctor said he thought it might be mono. That was the word they used. Mono. Then it didn't make sense with what they were seeing, and they looked again, and it was an inoperable brainstem tumor. His brother died not long after. Daniel was seven. He said he didn't understand the finality of it – he thought his brother would just come back in a week or two. He said it felt like a party, with the whole family together, people bringing food, and everyone being so kind to him. He didn't understand why it was a party until much later.

FOR YOU

Daniel said for a long time his identity was tied to being the kid
whose brother died.

He knows now that the identity was protecting him –
keeping him from having to grieve
what he didn't have the tools to grieve.

If you are carrying something you were too young to
understand when it happened,
the confusion was appropriate.

You were young.

You were supposed to be confused.

The grief is still there.

It kept.

DANIEL R.

The Mono That
Wasn't Mono

NINA R.

Are You Sitting Down?

She had told her father: you stress me out when you call because it always sounds like something is wrong. Could we have a code phrase? Something you only say if it's actually serious? They agreed on four words: *are you sitting down?* One day she was mid-conversation with someone when her phone rang. Her father said the words. She was distracted, still caught in the other conversation. She said: *no, why?* And it didn't click. Not yet. Then he said what he said. She still cannot say those words out loud. Her brother was gone.

FOR YOU

Nina and her father built a system
to protect her from exactly this moment –
and the moment arrived anyway,
wrapped in the very phrase they had chosen for it,
at exactly the wrong time to land.

Some things we try to prepare for cannot be prepared for.

The code phrase didn't fail.

The moment was just too large
for any container they could have made.

Whatever you are carrying from a call you weren't ready for –
you couldn't have been ready.

No one is.

NINA R.

Are You Sitting Down?

JOHN U.

We Turned Right Instead of Left

December 1st, 2007. Noon on a Saturday. His wife was usually at the jewelry store during the holiday season, but she was with them for once. They were leaving a swim meet, and their four-year-old son had behaved, so they'd promised him a Christmas tree. They turned right on the way home instead of left – to look at the holiday decorations at a prep school they passed. On a 55-mile undivided straightaway, a car crossed the center line. No skid marks. The police report put the impact speed at 125 miles an hour. John bled out four times in the first 12 hours. He was 36 years old. A 3% chance of survival. Eighteen days in a coma. He survived, and then spent the next 17 years having surgery after surgery, in pain without narcotics, a left leg that has felt asleep every day since, and a hole between the ventricles of his heart that no one had ever seen before.

FOR YOU

The other driver died at the scene.

John spent years with the question of why he survived
and the other man didn't.

A pastor friend eventually said:
maybe you just survived so your kids have a dad.

Maybe it's that simple.

John decided to let it be that simple.

That's not denial –
it's a choice about what to carry and what to put down.

Most of us are still deciding what to carry
from the worst thing that happened to us.

You're allowed to put some of it down.

JOHN U.

We Turned Right
Instead of Left

AVA J.

He Ran Three Stoplights

The night before, they had watched fireworks by the river in Louisville, her dad and her little brother on a scooter together, her mom and her on their own. It was July 4th. The day after, July 5th, they were walking to dinner when they stopped at a crosswalk. A man on fentanyl ran three stoplights at 50 miles an hour and hit her mother, her father, and her. Her little brother wasn't hit. Her mother flew 118 feet. Ava and her father flew 8 feet into the windshield. She was 17. Her older brother, who had been at a track meet, was the one who got the call. Ava was in a medically induced coma for 10 days, and her mother for 13. July 7th, her brother had to make the decision. Her father had donated his liver and kidneys and saved three people's lives. Ava woke up and had to relearn how to walk and talk. She didn't know any of it yet.

FOR YOU

Ava told me she doesn't want to be the version of herself who existed before the accident.

She loves this Ava –
the one who has been through it.

The one who knows what fireworks the night before an ordinary dinner actually means.

Most of us are walking to dinner right now, somewhere.

We don't know what we're walking toward.

That's not a reason to be afraid.

It's a reason to watch the fireworks.

AVA J.

He Ran Three Stoplights

RACHEL F.

The Message Turned Green

Her husband had flown to Tampa for a work lunch and was on his way home when he texted: *something happened on the plane.* She didn't understand. He repeated it. She called him. He couldn't answer – they were trying to land. And then he sent two final texts: *I love you and I love the girls.* She waited. She called his family. She called his brother, who flies planes, and could hear in his voice that he already knew. And when she hung up and looked at her phone and texted Matt again, the iMessage was green. On an iPhone, blue is iMessage. Green is a text to someone who can no longer receive it. She knew.

FOR YOU

Rachel said she kept hoping for a different response –
kept telling herself, give it a minute, give it an hour, he'll call.

The knowing and the hoping existed at the same time.

That coexistence – knowing and still hoping –
is one of the most human things there is.

Most of us will be asked to hold both at once someday.

There is no way to prepare for it.

You just hold both for as long as you can.

RACHEL F.

The Message Turned Green

VISO

She Said She'd Be Right Back

He was ten years old. His mother dropped him and his younger brother at the bowling alley near their house – a place they knew, less than a mile from home – and told them she'd be back in an hour. The owner knew the family. She left. An hour passed. Then more. The owner called their house. The nanny came to get them. They walked home. That night, their father showed up and said there had been an accident. He took them to stay with their cousins for the weekend. On Monday, he called them into his room and told them their mother had started a journey she was never coming back from. Viso's brother was seven. He went to bed. Three weeks later, a cousin showed Viso a newspaper clipping. His mother had died by suicide in a hotel room. He was ten years old and had been waiting at a bowling alley.

FOR YOU

Viso said he cried a lot after.

He talked about it constantly, to everyone,
until it became a thing that happened
rather than a thing that destroyed.

He said nothing that has happened since has ever been worse
– and so almost nothing else has been able to take him down
for long.

That's not a formula.

Most of us won't find our way through the way he did.

But the invitation in his story is still real:
what if the worst thing that happened to you
was also the thing that taught you how to live?

VISO

She Said
She'd Be Right Back

section 2

WHEN THE MOMENT WAS QUIET

Some lines in the sand are loud. You hear them coming. You feel them land.

And some arrive quietly.

In a parking lot before anyone else shows up.
In a theater where nothing sad is happening.
At a typewriter on an ordinary night.
In the dark, on a couch, on a bike, at the edge of a resignation letter you hadn't written yet.

Quiet doesn't mean small.
Quiet doesn't mean gradual.
It means the moment chose a different door.

These are still lines in the sand. Every single one. They still split everything into before and after. They still changed everything.

They just arrived without warning.

ROBERT N.

I Chose to Refuse the Order

It was 1970, and his deployment orders to Vietnam had come. He had been in the military, training with security air police, going through exercises for how to suppress demonstrations – and thinking, quietly, that if a real demonstration came, he would probably throw down his weapon and join the other side. When the orders arrived, he saw three paths: flee to Canada, refuse the order and face a court-martial with up to five years in a military prison and a dishonorable discharge, or go to war. He chose to refuse. He was court-martialed. He went to a military prison. He came out and spent the rest of his life in motion – itinerant labor, cooking, eventually Japan, where he has lived ever since.

FOR YOU

Robert said his strategic choice of words during the court-
martial saved him four and a half years.

He had thought carefully about what he believed and how to
say it – and that clarity, arrived at under pressure,
changed the shape of his sentence.

Sometimes, the most important preparation you can do
for the hardest moment
is to know, clearly and in advance,
what you actually believe.

Robert knew.

That knowing was the thing that carried him through.

ROBERT N.

I Chose to Refuse the Order

MATT G.

3:15 p.m., September 1st, 1989

I threw a fit about my mother going on a motorcycle trip. Nobody listened, because why would they. I was at day camp in Georgia when my father's boss's wife picked me up early, which was wrong, and everything about the quiet hallway was wrong, and my father sat me down and said the thing that split my life into before and after. My mother was gone.

FOR YOU

The moment doesn't have to be loud
to be the one that changes everything.

Sometimes it's just a quiet hallway
and a parent sitting down.

You probably know where your line is.

You probably know the before and the after.

That's not a wound.

That's a map.

MATT G.

3:15 p.m.,
September 1st, 1989

PETER B.

The Beer at the Typewriter

He was twenty-two years old, alone at a typewriter, a beer beside him, writing going nowhere. He had been in the same slow freefall for years – drinking too much, making a mess of things, trying to find the bottom so he could push off from it. That night at the typewriter, something shifted. Not a lightning bolt. More like the moment a fever finally breaks. He was sick and tired of being sick and tired, and this time he meant it.

FOR YOU

Most rock bottoms don't announce themselves.

They arrive quietly,
in an ordinary room,
on an ordinary night,
when you are just tired enough to finally stop.

If you have ever had a moment
where something in you said no more
and actually meant it –
that was the moment.

It counts even if nobody else saw it.

PETER B.

The Beer at the Typewriter

BRIAN A.

Seven Houses Away

He had spent a decade inside the LDS church – not as a believer but as someone who had chosen faith over doubt and then genuinely found something in it. He served on the bishopric. He was a high priest group leader. He coached lacrosse with the same people for eight years. He spent twenty to thirty hours a week, side by side, with 350 families who were his neighbors, his community, his life. Then he began to question, and to research, and to step away. And overnight – his word – every single one of them stopped. His phone went quiet. Nobody reached out. He could see them from his window. One family lived seven houses away. He had thought they were real friends. He never heard from them again.

FOR YOU

Brian said the depression that followed lasted years.

It wasn't just leaving a religion –
it was losing an entire world that had been built inside it.

Most of us will never experience that specific loss.

But most of us know what it is
to discover that a relationship was conditional
in a way we hadn't understood.

The silence of seven houses away
is a particular kind of grief.

You don't stop loving the people
just because they've stopped showing up.

BRIAN A.

Seven Houses Away

ANDREW L.

The Pitch-Black Neighborhood

For years, he had been stacking – teaching, union rep, holding students' trauma in five-minute passing periods, trying to fix everything at home the same way he fixed everything at work. One night on the couch with his partner, something boiled over. He stood up fast, said I gotta go, and exploded out the front door onto his bike. He rode as hard as he could until his body gave out. He found himself forty blocks away in a neighborhood he didn't recognize, no streetlights, straddling the bike in the dark, just breathing. And for the first time, a thought arrived that had never come before: *maybe I don't have to fix everything. Maybe it's not all mine.*

FOR YOU

Andrew said he wished he had known how to cry before that night –
that the energy might have had somewhere to go.

Most of us were never taught that either.

But the body knows what the mind won't admit,
and sometimes it has to get you forty blocks away in the dark
before it can finally say the thing out loud.

If you are carrying more than is yours to carry,
you already know it.

The question is just when you'll let yourself
put some of it down.

ANDREW L.

The Pitch-Black Neighborhood

DEBRA M. & STEVE Z.

What Do I Do Now, Who Am I Now?

Three years after her stroke, Deb was still fighting to get back to Stanford. She had worked relentlessly – in the gym, on the stretching table, doing the work – because she and Steve both believed it was only a matter of time. Then her medical team told her she had to give up her professorship. She said it out loud for the first time: *my identity theft*. Steve said that was the moment they both accepted that life was changed forever – not just her career, but how she would be a parent, a wife, a daughter. It got dark. And then, being Deb, she decided to write a book. Because professors write books. She would show them.

> **FOR YOU**
>
> Deb didn't choose to lose her professorship.
>
> It was taken.
>
> What she chose – the writing, the nonprofit, the showing up
> anyway – came after.
>
> That's the part that's available to all of us.
>
> We don't always get to choose what is taken from us.
>
> We do get to choose what we build
> in the space it leaves behind.

DEBRA M. & STEVE Z.

What Do I Do Now, Who Am I Now?

DAY 5.

The Impulse Into the Woods

His father died after four years of cancer. His relationship ended around the same time. He could barely work, barely socialize, barely take care of his house. He adopted his father's dog – a miniature schnauzer named Rudy – and she got him outside, across the threshold, when grief alone would have kept him under the covers. One morning at dawn, months after his father died, they were on a long walk through the regional park when they came upon a crossroads of three paths converging. Something in him stopped. He knelt down, gathered what was at his feet – leaves, stones, whatever was there – and made something small on the ground. He didn't know what he was doing. He just followed the impulse.

FOR YOU

Day calls grief a skill, not an emotion.

What he found at that crossroads
was a way to presence his loss instead of outrun it –
to make something with his hands
that told the story his words couldn't hold.

You don't have to go to the woods.

You don't have to make anything.

But if there is something you have been carrying
that you haven't yet found a way to say,

it might be worth asking what form it wants to take.

The grief is already doing something inside you.

You might as well give it a shape.

DAY 5.

The Impulse
Into the Woods

JOHN D.

I Packed Two Bags

His mother had been drinking and using painkillers for years – it started after she broke her spine and was prescribed opioids, and it spiraled from there. He watched it happen from nineteen to twenty-seven. He came home from the army, and things were worse. Most nights, he kept weapons in his room and locked the door because she would come after him. He still loved her. He still had their mornings. Then one morning she came at him, and he looked in her eyes, and she was sober, and she still wasn't there. He packed everything he owned into two bags, laid out his terms clearly, and left. He had no money. He had no support system. Nobody knew what had been happening inside that house for eight years. He had never asked anyone for help. He had believed that's what men do.

FOR YOU

John said leaving was nearly impossible
because you can't make a string of good decisions
when you're in crisis.

But he made one.

He packed two bags and walked out.

Sometimes one decision is enough.

You don't have to have the whole plan.

You just have to make the next right move.

JOHN D.

I Packed Two Bags

ELLEN B.

Crying in the Dark

She had come straight from work to meet her husband and daughter for dinner, which always felt a little sad – she hadn't gotten to go with them. They ate, then went to see Beetlejuice, which was in a touring Broadway production. A great musical. Not a sad musical. The lights went down, and Ellen started crying, and could not stop. She was sitting there in the dark next to her family, sobbing through a comedy about death, with no explanation and no ability to make it stop. Her husband leaned over. *What is wrong with you?* She didn't know. She had been crying on the way into work and on the way home from work for months, and she hadn't let herself understand why. In the dark, her body finally said what her mind had been refusing to.

FOR YOU

Ellen had spent years giving everything she had to everyone else –
her team, her workplace, her family –
and leaving nothing for herself.

The body keeps a ledger even when
the mind refuses to look at it.

If you have ever broken down somewhere you didn't expect,
in front of something that had no right to break you –
that wasn't weakness.
That was your body telling you the truth
you'd been too busy to hear.

It knew before you did.

It usually does.

ELLEN B.

Crying in the Dark

GINNY P.

The Ding of the Email

She had just come home from a ten-day trip to Italy with her partner. She traveled for work almost every week, but this one felt different on the way back. A friend texted her mid-travel day: *what time do you land? Can you meet me for a cocktail?* They were not Tuesday-night-cocktail friends. Something was wrong. Ginny spent the whole day trying to figure out how to be a good friend to someone in trouble. She walked into the restaurant at 10 p.m. to find her friend shaking and sobbing over an empty glass. The friend had information. She had a list. Ginny, skeptical, went home and made one phone call – to a hotel in the Twin Cities, asking if her partner had a stay on record that day. They put her on hold. She sat on the edge of the bed. The clerk came back: *I've got that receipt right here, where should I send it?* When the email dinged, she felt like she'd been kicked in the stomach. She ran to the bathroom.

FOR YOU

Ginny said the whole day
she was trying to figure out how to show up for someone else.

She had no idea she was walking toward her own life.

The ding of an email
shouldn't be the sound that ends a chapter.

But sometimes that's what it is.

If something in you already knows the answer,
you already know the answer.

GINNY P.

The Ding of the Email

LAUREN L.

She Couldn't Unsee It

She had been working in her family's business for years – a predetermined path, secure, expected. She had been trying to say she needed to leave. Her mother kept saying they would figure it out. They went downhill. Then one Fall, around Halloween, something happened at her desk, and she broke. She was hunched over, sobbing, and her mother was in the room and saw it – really saw it – for the first time. Lauren said: *I don't want to be here anymore.* And in that moment, her mother accepted it. It was time for Lauren to go. It was a reality, she said, that her mother couldn't unsee.

FOR YOU

Lauren had been saying the words for a long time before that moment.

The words hadn't been enough.

What finally changed things wasn't a new argument or a
better case – it was being seen, fully and visibly,
in the actual state she was in.

Sometimes we have to stop managing how we appear
and let someone witness how we actually are.

The breakdown at the desk was not a failure.

It was the thing that finally made the truth undeniable.

LAUREN L.

She Couldn't Unsee It

LIN Y.

The Building Looked Like a Black Hole

She arrived before anyone else. No one had told her to. She was the first manager ever on site, proof to herself of how seriously she was taking this promotion she hadn't wanted. It was a perfect summer morning in Canada. Blue sky. No clouds. She sat alone in an empty parking lot staring at the building door, and it looked like a black hole. She thought: *I don't know if I'm going to survive the day.* And then she started sobbing – full body, uncontrollable – the kind she would only later understand was probably clinical depression she had never named. She cried until she heard herself think: *your coworkers are going to arrive soon and they cannot see this.* She grabbed a tissue, fixed her makeup, and walked in. She handed in her resignation six months later.

FOR YOU

Lin grew up in China being beaten by parents
who were beaten by their own parents,
trained by a culture that said survival is the same as success,
and had spent 20 years in Canada trying to prove it.

The parking lot was the morning her body said: no more.

Not to the job – to all of it.

To the pattern that said you have to earn your place,
show up early, be the best, never let them see.

She didn't know that yet, sitting there with the tissue.

But her body knew.

Yours does too.

LIN Y.

The Building Looked
Like a Black Hole

HEATHER T.

A Whole Pack on the Patio

She had been married for sixteen years when her husband walked out of a therapy session and didn't come back. She drove straight to her parents' house, stopping on the way to buy a pack of cigarettes – she hadn't smoked since college. She sat on her parents' back patio and told them everything. They didn't know a thing. Nobody did. She had been living in a bubble so complete that not even the people closest to her had seen the cracks forming. Over the next four hours, she smoked the entire pack, chain cigarette by chain cigarette, saying out loud for the first time everything she had been carrying alone.

FOR YOU

Heather said she had no choice in the matter
other than to figure out how to react.

That's actually the whole thing.

The choice we make in the moment the ground gives way –
not whether to feel it,
but what to do with it once we do.

She drove to her parents.

She sat down.

She said the things.

That was the beginning.

Sometimes the most important decision
you make in the worst moment
is just the one that gets you out of the car.

HEATHER T.

A Whole Pack on the Patio

section 3

WHAT THE BODY KNOWS

The body has its own timeline.

It absorbs what the mind refuses,
stores what we push past,
speaks in a language we only learn to read after the fact.

Illness. Injury. The panic that won't leave.

The moment you pull into a garage and sit with the car running, making a list of reasons to stay.

The body makes decisions the mind hasn't caught up to yet.

I've come to believe that the body is always trying to tell us something.

The stories in this section are about the moments when people finally had to listen.

PARIS S.

Court-Ordered

She had been assaulted at fifteen and buried it. For years, she ran – kept moving, kept achieving, kept distracting herself with the next thing, telling herself that as long as she stayed in motion, she would never have to deal with it. She was nineteen when her body finally stopped her. She broke down and was taken first to an urgent psychiatric center, then transported to a hospital, and then court-ordered into treatment. She was terrified. She said it was the scariest experience of her life – those rooms, that stillness, nowhere left to run.

FOR YOU

Paris said she thought she could outrun it.

A lot of us believe that.

We think motion is the same as okay.
We think busy means healed.
But the body keeps its own timeline,
and it will eventually choose the moment to stop you –
not to break you,
but to make you deal with what you've been carrying
since the moment you first decided not to.

Whatever you've been running from is still there.

You don't have to wait until you're court-ordered to stop.

PARIS S.

Court-Ordered

CHRIS M.

The Night the Mind He Trusted Fell Apart

On an ordinary evening in 2017, a small piece of a cannabis edible triggered a full psychotic episode. Chris ran barefoot into his front yard, smashing his head into the bushes, trying to silence voices no one else could hear. Neighbors called the police. He fought them because he couldn't recognize who they were. He ended up zip-tied on the ground. He woke up the next morning on the other side of a door he hadn't known was there.

FOR YOU

There is something almost generous
about hitting a wall you can't think your way through.

Because it means the thing you've been using
to solve every problem
finally has to rest.

If you've ever felt like your own mind was working against you,
you are not broken.

You are just being asked to try something different.

CHRIS M.

The Night the Mind You Trusted Fell Apart

VANESSA A.

The Teacher Who Woke Up Without a Voice

She went to bed on a Wednesday feeling like she had a bad cold. Nauseous, a little off, the kind of thing you chalk up to a strange bug. Over the next seven days, it got worse. By the end of the week, she was in the ICU, intubated, her body going quiet in ways she couldn't explain or stop. She woke up unable to talk. A tracheostomy in her throat, a communication device in front of her, a speech pathologist standing at the foot of her bed, assessing her. Vanessa had spent her career giving people their voices. She was now the patient. She used her eyes to say what her mouth could not.

FOR YOU

Vanessa told me something
she had only recently figured out:
that six years later,
she still wakes up at one or two in the morning.

Every night.

She wondered if her body remembered that this was when it
all started –
when she went to the ER,
when the paralysis began,
when everything changed.

Her body had kept that time like a vigil,
like a sentinel that never got the all-clear.

The body doesn't forget what the mind tries to move past.

If yours is still keeping watch over something,
that's not weakness.

That's memory.

It's trying to protect you.

VANESSA A.

The Teacher Who Woke Up Without a Voice

DR. ROBB K.

The Night He Fell to His Knees in the Rain

He was on the streets of Manchester, soaking wet, out of money, out of options, out of road. He had been successful before the drinking took everything. That night, he fell to his knees in the rain and said the only thing left to say: if there's a God up there, I can't do this on my own. Thirty seconds later, a stranger appeared and asked if he needed help.

FOR YOU

Robb said that stranger saved his life.

But the thing that made that possible
was the falling to his knees –
the admission that he could not do it alone.

Most of us wait until we have no other option
before we say that out loud.

You don't have to wait that long.

Asking for help is not the last resort.

It can be the first move.

DR. ROBB K.

The Night He Fell to His Knees in the Rain

MORGAN G.

The Sound Machine

She had just put her newborn son down for a nap when she noticed the sound machine seemed to have gone silent. She turned to check – it was on. She leaned back down to kiss her son, looked up again, and thought it had stopped. It hadn't. She had lost all hearing in one ear, suddenly, completely. Doctors said sinus infection. Postpartum stress. She pushed for an audiologist, then an MRI. Two days after the scan, the nurse called and said: *there's something. I can't tell you more. You have to come in.* Morgan handed her records to a nurse friend while waiting. Her friend looked at them and started crying. Then the doctor said the words: *multiple sclerosis.* Morgan was thirty-six years old, with two small children, and had just moved to Italy with her military husband.

FOR YOU

Morgan said she kept being dismissed –
sinus infection, stress, postpartum.

She kept pushing anyway.

The body was telling her something true,
and she listened to it even when the people around her
weren't.

Whatever your body is telling you
that someone keeps explaining away,
it might be worth one more push.

You know your body.

Trust what it's saying.

MORGAN G.

The Sound Machine

ELIZABETH R.

The Migraine She Gave Herself

She loved her job. That's the thing she kept saying. She wasn't burned out because she hated what she was doing – she was burned out because she loved it too much to stop. She had been traveling the world, working with creative people, launching campaigns, finally feeling like an expert after years of building toward it. And then one day her body overrode all of it. A migraine so severe she lost all motor skills. She ended up in the emergency room convinced she was having a stroke or had a brain tumor. She wasn't. She had simply done too much for too long, and her body had decided it was done waiting to be heard.

FOR YOU

Elizabeth said burnout doesn't only happen when you hate
what you're doing.

Sometimes it happens because you love it –
because you gave it everything
and forgot to keep anything for yourself.

The body doesn't care how much you love the thing.

It just knows when the tank is empty.

If you are waiting for a sign that it's time to slow down,
this might be it.

ELIZABETH R.

The Migraine
She Gave Herself

DR. PIPER G.

The Doctor Said Spank Him

Her son had been jerking his neck, clapping his hands, blinking rapidly, unable to control his own bodily movements. Eight prescriptions. Ten doctors. Nothing working. Then the neurologist – no MRI, no blood work, no tests – watched her son lie on the floor for a few minutes and said: *I think he just needs a good spanking.* Piper looked at him. She said okay in the way you say okay when you are too stunned to say anything else. She walked out to the car. And then she decided.

FOR YOU

Piper said she knew in her mama's soul
that something else was going on.

She had known it through every appointment,
every dismissal,
every unhelpful answer.
The neurologist didn't create that knowing –
he just finally made it impossible to ignore.

You already know the things you know.

The question is how long you'll let someone else's authority
override what your body has been trying to tell you.

PIPER G.

The Doctor Said
Spank Him

ANASTASIA Z.

I Don't Want to Die. I Just Don't Want to Live This Way Anymore.

She had been managing depression and anxiety for most of her life – exercise, journaling, yoga, keeping it moving. Then the pandemic came, and the coping mechanisms stopped working. One afternoon, she got in her car and drove to a trail above the Pacific Ocean, leaving her phone behind. She walked toward the edge of something she had been circling for a long time. And then, somewhere on the trail, a glimmer. She thought about her children. She thought about what she would be ruining for them. She realized she didn't want to die. She just didn't want to live the way she had been living. She borrowed a phone from a stranger and texted her husband three words: *I am okay*. She knew it was the lie she had been telling her whole life. And she kept walking until her friend – sent by her husband, searching seven trails – came around a bend and grabbed her.

FOR YOU

Anastasia spent decades believing that needing help meant
she was flawed.

That the medication, the therapy, the asking –
all of it was evidence of something broken in her.

On that trail, she found out what was actually true:
she didn't want to die.

She wanted a different life.

Those are not the same thing.

If you are carrying something that feels too heavy to name,
please name it to someone.

The glimmer is real.
It was enough for her.
It might be enough for you, too.

ANASTASIA Z.

I Don't Want to Die. I Just Don't Want to Live This Way Anymore.

SCOTT M.

The Cat on His Shoulder

He woke up from a coma as a quadruple amputee. Then he spent three years fighting a ten-million-dollar malpractice lawsuit, only to lose. The day the verdict came in, he drove home, pulled into his garage, and sat there thinking about not turning off the car. He thought about it for a long time. Then he went upstairs. He put on music. His cat climbed onto his shoulder. And he made a list all night of everything he still had to live for.

FOR YOU

Scott didn't choose to lose his limbs.

He didn't choose to lose the lawsuit.

What he chose was to go upstairs.
To put on the music.
To let the cat sit on his shoulder.
To make the list.

The list didn't fix anything.

But it got him through the night.

Sometimes that's all a list has to do.

SCOTT M.

The Cat on His Shoulder

MICHELLE G.

If You Had Waited Until Friday

She celebrated her forty-first birthday at the beach on a Thursday. That Saturday night, she woke up with sharp back pain. Heating pad, Motrin, yoga positions from YouTube. By Monday, it was worse. She called her doctor. They said wait until Friday. Monday night, she shot up off the couch in the worst pain of her life and couldn't breathe. She still didn't go to the ER – the kids were asleep. She slept on the couch in thirty-minute intervals. By Tuesday morning, she told her husband: *Take me to the ER*. She punched her symptoms into the intake screen and was called back before she finished typing. Her lungs were filled with blood clots. She was having a pulmonary embolism. The ER doctor told her: *if you had waited until Friday to see your regular doctor, you would have died.*

FOR YOU

Michelle said after she was home and recovered,
her hematologist read the post-op report and asked:
do you still have the filter in your neck?

She had a scar to prove something had gone through her
neck.

The report didn't mention it.

She spent weeks chasing down a doctor
who had forgotten to document a procedure on her own
body.

The self-advocacy didn't end in the ER.

It never does.

If you have been dismissed, minimized,
or told to wait until Friday –
your instincts about your own body are data.

Treat them that way.

MICHELLE G.

If You Had Waited
Until Friday

BROOKS B.

Sadly, We Found a Tumor

She had been bleeding internally for two months, and two doctors had told her it was probably a hemorrhoid. She cold-called a gastroenterologist and convinced her to schedule a colonoscopy on New Year's Eve. She'd had a zombie costume ready for a party that night. She didn't go to the party. Four days later, she woke up from the procedure and saw the doctor's face before the doctor said a word. The doctor said: *sadly, we found a tumor, and it's almost certainly cancerous.* Brooks didn't cry. She was 38, the CEO of a company she'd built over 16 years, a woman who had already survived a stroke at 24 and spent her career learning to fix everything. She looked at the doctor and thought: *okay, I'll figure this out.* Then a nurse appeared in the doorway, cheerful and oblivious, and asked: *how are you doing, honey? Did they find some hemorrhoids?* Brooks was still lying there with the news.

FOR YOU

Brooks said the cancer was the best thing that ever happened
to her,
and she knows how that sounds.

She doesn't say it lightly.

She says it because the person on the other side –
the one who sleeps in, makes friends, follows her purpose,
laughs at ass jokes,
and finally feels the joy she spent 16 years producing but
never quite having –
that person required something to break the old one open.

Whatever has arrived in your life that you didn't want:
it might be doing the same.

BROOKS B.

Sadly, We Found a Tumor

REBECCA L.

More Scalp Than Hair

She had always had thin hair – the kind that couldn't hold the big 80s bangs, couldn't fill a proper ballet bun, couldn't be ignored forever. In January 2019, after a year of divorce proceedings, moving three times, and working late into the night, she was out with friends, and someone took photos. The next day, she looked at them online and saw more scalp than hair. She started Googling, then went to Instagram instead, and found communities of women in their twenties and thirties who had chosen to own their hair loss rather than hide it. She followed them, slid into some of their DMs, and asked questions. And slowly the idea shifted: this didn't have to be something to run from. She bought a topper. Then a second, with more hair. She learned to wear it and then to love it. And some days now she doesn't wear anything at all.

FOR YOU

Rebecca said the women she found online kept telling her:
nobody really cares what you're doing
as long as it doesn't affect them negatively.

That sounds cynical.

It's actually liberating.

The story you've been telling yourself
about what other people see and judge and think –
most of them aren't telling that story.

You're the only one who has been living inside it.

REBECCA L.

More Scalp Than Hair

section 4

THE IMPOSSIBLE DECISION

Some shifts aren't done to you.

You do them yourself.

You make the choice, and then you live inside the choice
and you don't always know, at the moment of making it,
what it will cost or what it will open.

You just know you have to decide.

There is something specific about the weight of a decision
you can't undo.

The people in this section made choices that rewrote
everything after them –
a birth, a last show, a phone call made and not taken back,
a door left open, a door closed for good.

They knew, or came to know, that the weight was the point.
The weight meant it mattered.

TRYSTAN R.

The Birth

Trystan is a transgender man. He carried his son and gave birth to him. In a single moment, every fixed idea about what a body can do, what a family can look like, what it means to be a man and a father and a person – all of it became something larger and stranger and more alive than any category had room for.

FOR YOU

Most of us will never be asked to redefine the terms the way
Trystan was.

But the underlying question –
can I be all of these things at once,
can I hold what seems contradictory and still know who I am –
is one a lot of us are living with.

Trystan's answer was yes.

The body already knew.

TRYSTAN R.

The Birth

SETH S.

The Moment the Silence Got Louder Than the Stage

He had spent his career moving between Broadway and the wilderness – doing a show, then disappearing into the woods for months to learn primitive skills and sit around fires with strangers, then coming back to do another show. He had been living this duality for years. Then, mid-run on his last Broadway contract, he heard what he calls his higher voice: *this is your last show*. He didn't tell anyone. He had three or four months left. He finished the run, didn't renew, and left for seven years. He went to Peru, to Mount Shasta, to jungles and mountains. He followed the voice that had been speaking to him since he was eighteen and finally decided to stop scheduling around it.

FOR YOU

Seth said he had always lived between worlds.

The wilderness called him, and the stage called him
and for a long time he answered both.

What changed was when he stopped treating the deeper call
as the thing he'd get to eventually
and made it the thing.

Most of us have a version of that voice.

The question is what we keep putting
between ourselves and the moment we finally listen.

SETH S.

The Moment the Silence Got Louder Than the Stage

LYDIA K.

The Call

She had built one of the top health coaching practices in the world while secretly living with a life-threatening eating disorder. For years, she ran the double life – thousands of clients, a team of coaches, a public image of health – while locking herself in her bedroom closet to cry where no one could hear her. One night on the closet floor, she considered not going on. And then something shifted: *what if this is a habit, not a disease? What if I can deprogram from this the same way I deprogrammed from the cult?* A few weeks later, she was on a national call. Thousands of people tuned in expecting health tips. She decided she couldn't do it anymore. She told them the truth.

FOR YOU

Lydia said the closet floor
was where her brain finally opened to solutions she hadn't
considered before –
because she had given up on the ones that weren't working.

Sometimes we have to exhaust every familiar option
before we're willing to try something that feels impossible.

The darkness was not the end of her story.

It was the moment before the door.

LYDIA K.

The Call

JONATHAN G.

His Daughter Had Just Been Born

He had been running fast – fast money, fast decisions, fast trouble. He gave a false name in a Pennsylvania courtroom and sat behind the door waiting for his arraignment. When the officers came in high-fiving each other, something in him said *go*. He made it all the way back to California on a bus. And then his daughter was born. He and his fiancée had a long conversation. He said: *I have to turn myself in.* He called. He made arrangements. He walked back in. He did eighteen months in a Pennsylvania state penitentiary. He went in knowing his daughter was out there. He came out with a different life.

FOR YOU

Jonathan said his daughter had just been born
when he made the decision to face what he had done.

Not the arrest.
Not the courtroom.
Not the escape.
His daughter.

The moment something you love more than your freedom
exists in the world, the calculation changes.

Whatever it is that is asking you to be accountable –
to walk back in, to face the thing you ran from –
the people who love you are already waiting on the other side.

JONATHAN G.

His Daughter
Had Just Been Born

MATT G.

He Laid Down on His Own

Mikey had been pacing for months – walking circles around the house, getting stuck in corners, unable to stop moving or lie down on his own. Thirty minutes before the vet arrived, he came over to where we were sitting on the floor. He sat between us. And then he laid down on his own for the first time in a long time, put his head in my hands, and was still.

FOR YOU

If I hadn't had that moment,
the guilt would have been harder to survive.

Mikey gave me a gift in those last thirty minutes –
not a resolution, not an answer,
but a confirmation.

Sometimes, the thing we most need before a loss
is just a moment of quiet that says:
this is right, and I am loved, and I am ready.

We don't always get that.

I did.

I am still grateful.

MATT G.

He Laid Down on His Own

NICOLE M.

Put Him Down

She had gone from Catholic school and strict parents to a whirlwind engagement and a marriage that moved fast – too fast to see the control for what it was. Her dream of law school and the United Nations was told no. She stayed. Then one afternoon she was outside with her daughter when her then-husband went to the kitchen, grabbed their two-year-old son out of his high chair, and started shaking him – threatening to throw him in the pool, threatening to drown him. Her son was pounding on his father's chest screaming *put me down daddy, put me down*. She grabbed her daughter, ran for the home phone, and called 911.

FOR YOU

Nicole said she had been raised so sheltered
that she expected other people to be like her.

She had to learn, over and over, that they weren't.

The moment her son was in that man's arms
was the moment the lesson finally
cost too much to keep learning.

If you are in a situation
where you keep telling yourself it will get better –
listen to what your body already knows.

You don't have to wait until someone else is in danger
to trust what you've been feeling.

NICOLE M.

Put Him Down

CHERYL W.

California Dreamin'

She was twenty years old, living the restaurant life in Wilmington, North Carolina, a long way from California. A friend called late and talked her into going out – she was a homebody, never a bar person, but she went. They hopped three bars, danced, had a great time. When they walked back to the car, he tossed her the keys. She threw them back. He threw them again. By the time they got to the car, he was already in the passenger seat, and she got in and started driving. They were listening to California Dreamin. Twenty, thirty blocks of stop signs and back streets. Then a left-hand curve. She lost control. The inertia took them into a pole – right into the passenger side door. She opened her eyes and stared at the steering wheel. She looked over. Her friend was slumped on the center console. She pleaded with him to wake up, told him they had to get out. He didn't move. She leaned over and could hear that he was breathing – a curdling sound, saliva and blood. She got out and stood next to the car. She could hear sirens in the distance. She went to jail that night.

FOR YOU

Cheryl said shame is weirdly comfortable –
much easier to live in than forgiveness.

She spent thirty years practicing her way
toward forgiving herself.

What she found on the other side was not absolution
but something more durable:
the understanding that carrying it honestly
is different from being crushed by it.

Whatever you did that you can't put down,
the question isn't whether you deserve to be free of it.

It's whether you're willing to do the work
of making something out of the weight.

CHERYL W.

California Dreamin

DR. TONY D.

If You Could Hear a Spirit Break

He had been a Navy SEAL. He had run toward fires when everyone else ran away. He had trained his whole life to be the guy people called when everything went wrong. And on a three-day bender, the daycare called. There had been an H1N1 exposure, and someone needed to come pick up his son. His wife was out of the area. He tried to get out of the room. He couldn't. For three hours, he tried to get off that bed and go be the father his son needed, and he could not do it. He turned off his phone. He pushed it under the bed. He kept using. He said: *if you could hear a spirit break, that was it.* He knew what he was. About a month later, he was in someone else's house at 3 a.m., and he looked into the eyes of a 13-year-old kid and saw no innocence there. He saw what his own son was going to become. He went downstairs, found a phone book, and started calling treatment centers. The Farley Center had a bed. He took it.

FOR YOU

Tony spent nine years telling himself he could quit if he
wanted to.

He just didn't want to.

The phone under the bed
was the moment every lie he had told himself
stopped working at the same time.

He was a man trained to be a hero
who could not get out of a room.

The recovery didn't start with a brilliant decision.

It started with a phone book at 3 a.m. and one phone call.

You don't have to be ready.

You just have to make the call.

DR. TONY D.

If You Could
Hear a Spirit Break

SEAN W.

They're Gonna Hate That They Gave Me This Much Time to Think

He was seventeen, sitting next to his attorney in the courtroom, as the judge read out numbers he didn't fully understand. Then he heard one sentence that cut through: *Sean Wilson, you will be able to contribute to our society in your mid-thirties.* He leaned over and asked his attorney: *what is she saying?* His attorney patted his arm and said he'd explain in the back. Sean sat back. And the thought that came to him, the one that changed everything: *they are gonna hate that they gave me this much time to think.* He didn't know yet how much time it was. He just knew he had some.

FOR YOU

Sean said he didn't know, in that moment,
which way it would go.

That thought could have fueled rage
just as easily as it fueled him.

What made the difference was the decision,
made in a courtroom at seventeen,
that this was not his life –
and that whatever time he had been given,
he was going to use it.

Most of us will never face anything like what Sean faced.

But the question underneath his story is one we all carry:
when the thing you cannot change has already happened,
what do you decide to do with the time?

SEAN W.

They're Gonna Hate That They Gave Me This Much Time to Think

section 5

WHAT SOMEONE SAID

A sentence.

Sometimes that's all it takes.

The right one at the right time, or the wrong one,
or the one that simply named a truth
that had been living in the room without a name.

You hear it, and something in you shifts –
not because the words are extraordinary,
but because they are finally, exactly true.

I've been collecting sentences for years on this podcast
without quite knowing that's what I was doing.

Every conversation has one.

A thing someone said that split before from after.
The entries in this section are organized around that moment
– the sentence, and what it did.

JILLIAN C.

Just Go

Her partner was shaking as he confessed. She was still in love with him. She stood there in freeze mode, stone cold, her dog pressing against her leg, the only one in the room moving. She didn't know what to do. The only thing she could think of was to call her mother. She put the phone on speaker and told her everything. Then she said: *Mom, I think I have to leave. I really think I have to leave right now.* Her mother said two words: *Jillian, just go.* She went.

FOR YOU

Jillian said it was the scariest moment of her life.

She was still in love with him in that moment.

Both things were true at the same time.

The love didn't make the leaving wrong –
it made it harder,
which is not the same thing.

If you are waiting for the feeling of loving someone
to go away before you make a decision about them,
you may wait a very long time.

Sometimes the bravest thing
is to go while you still love them.

JILLIAN C.

Just Go

MATT G.

Every Decision Since Then Has Been Made by That Scared Eight-Year-Old

I was in my thirties, in a therapist's office, working through what I thought were ordinary adult problems, when she stopped me and said the thing that split my understanding of myself in two. Every decision you've made since your mother died has been made by that scared eight-year-old. I had been living that way for twenty years without knowing it.

FOR YOU

Most of us have a version of this –
an age we got stuck at,
a fear we've been making decisions from,
a wound that's been running the show
without our knowledge.

You don't have to know what yours is right now.

But if there's a pattern in your life that doesn't make sense,
if you keep arriving at the same place by different roads,
it might be worth asking
who inside you is still making the call.

MATT G.

Every Decision Since Then Has Been Made
by That Scared Eight-Year-Old

KYLE R.

What the Teacher Said

He was in his sixth year of high school, assigned to in-school suspension, when the teacher running the room got to know him. One day, his teacher took him aside. He told Kyle he was smart. That he could do something with his life. Kyle said it blew his mind – because it was the first time anyone had taken the time to say that to him. He had grown up with a stepfather who called him a loser. He thought all men were like that. His teacher was the first one who wasn't.

FOR YOU

Kyle's teacher didn't know he was changing a life.

He was just being himself,
paying attention to a kid in a room.

You probably remember someone
who said something to you at the right moment
that you still carry.

And you probably don't realize
how many people
are still carrying something you said to them.

The words land whether you know it or not.

KYLE R.

What the Teacher Said

NEWTON C.

I Don't Know How to Turn This Around

It was a pandemic-era team meeting on video. Everyone was in their little thumbnails. A friend had nudged him in the chat before the check-in: *say something real*. When it got to Newton, he didn't know where he would go with it. And then, without entirely planning to, he started to cry. He said: *right now I'm struggling, because the number of days I'm proud of how I'm showing up as a father is going down, and I don't know how to turn that around*. Two things hit him at once: the horror of having said it in front of his coworkers, and the recognition that he had never said it that clearly even to himself. He heard it and knew it was true. He couldn't unsee it.

FOR YOU

Newton said once those words were out,

he couldn't take them back.

And he was terrified.

And it was also the beginning of everything getting better.

There is something that you know is true

that you haven't said out loud yet –

maybe not even to yourself.

The saying of it is frightening.

It is also what makes it possible to do something about it.

NEWTON C.

I Don't Know
How to Turn This Around

HEATHER T.

The Word That Finally Fit

For years, she had been switching jobs because she was bored, struggling to focus, dragging herself through corporate days, being told she had anxiety when she knew she didn't. She was a writer and director working in advertising to survive as she immigrated between two countries. Therapists kept putting her in boxes that didn't fit. She kept wondering why someone as capable as she knew herself to be couldn't just get through the day. She began to suspect ADHD. She was afraid to name it – she had internalized the idea that you couldn't be intelligent and have a disability. Then a doctor she trusted said the words out loud. The diagnosis wasn't a label that diminished her. It was the first time anyone had accurately described what had always been true.

FOR YOU

Heather said she had been erasing the difficult parts of her own story
to maintain the belief that she was fine.

The diagnosis didn't create a problem.

It named one that had always been there.

If you have been trying to outperform a thing you haven't yet named,
named,
naming it is not defeat.

It is the beginning of actually dealing with it.

HEATHER T.

The Word That Finally Fit

ANDREW M.

Do You Believe in Angels?

It was a Wednesday morning, nothing special. He was serving tables in Nashville, and a mother and daughter sat down. He brought them something – a margarita pizza, he thinks – and ended up in a conversation he couldn't stop. His coming out. His music. His complicated relationship with God, family, and the church he'd left. They were both crying at the table. Her daughter was across from them, probably wondering what was happening to her server. The mother had just lost her husband and written a book about it. She asked Andrew about his music. He told her about the songs he hadn't released yet, just sitting on his hard drive. She looked at him and said: *whatever you have, the world needs to hear it now.* He got her name and her daughter's name. They left. He went home and spent over an hour searching the internet. He could not find either of them. Nothing. He texted his best friend: *do you believe in angels? Because I think I just talked to one.* The next song went viral.

FOR YOU

Andrew said that the stranger validated everything he had
risked – leaving the PhD, coming out,
dropping everything to move to Nashville alone.

One sentence from a woman
he can't find anywhere on the internet
confirmed what he had been trying to believe about himself.

You probably have a sentence someone said to you that did
the same thing.

You're allowed to let it count.

ANDREW M.

Do You Believe in Angels?

HEIDI K.

My Dad Doesn't Do That

She was a month into her marriage when she got drunk enough to be picked up by a cop who drove her home. Her husband was furious. Her dad was furious. She was defiant – they hadn't arrested her, what was the big deal? Then her father said the thing that cracked it open: *you have a problem, and you need to figure it out*. And then he went quiet. That was the thing. Her dad didn't do that. He didn't interject in her adult life. If he was saying it, there was probably a problem. The next morning, her husband had a softball game. She felt too awful from the night before to sit in the sun. She stayed in the car and looked up how to get sober. The next day, she went to AA.

FOR YOU

Heidi said the right person said the right sentence at the right
time – and it only landed because of who said it.

Her father's silence over the years
is what gave his words their weight.

The people in your life who speak rarely
but mean it when they do –
listen to them.

They've been watching.

They know something.

HEIDI K.

My Dad Doesn't Do That

CHANTAL W.

The Letter on the Desk

She had been bullied so severely in high school that she finally reached a breaking point – she was going to drop out and do virtual school alone at home. The day before she left, she broke down in her English teacher's classroom. The teacher shut the door, closed the blinds, and sat with her while she unloaded everything she had been carrying. He talked her into staying one more day. Then he told her about a poetry scholarship contest – top three winners received two full years of college tuition – and asked her for three poems. She didn't think she had a chance. She gave him the poems and forgot about it. Months later, he called her into his class and put the letter on the desk in front of her. She had won the whole thing.

FOR YOU

Chantal said that one person finally stopped and listened,
and it completely changed the course of her life.

Her teacher didn't know that.
He was just being a teacher.

Most of the people who change our lives
don't know they're doing it.

If you are in a position to shut the door,
close the blinds,
and sit with someone who is carrying too much –
you might be writing a letter
they'll remember for the rest of their lives.

CHANTAL W.

The Letter on the Desk

KATHLEEN M.

Only 2.5 Percent

She was fifty-six years old, facilitating a trauma training in Kansas City, when the presenter put up the ACE data. Kathleen had calculated her own score as she went – a nine. But when she wrote it down, she wrote eight. She didn't want to be too far from the norm. Then the state data went up. Only 2.5 percent of people score eight, nine, or ten. She looked at the numbers. And for the first time in her life, she understood that not everyone grew up the way she did. She had spent fifty-six years thinking that everybody has a lot of stuff to deal with.

FOR YOU

Kathleen said that moment gave her language.
It gave her science.

It gave her permission to begin healing.

For decades, she had been steeled up, driving forward,
operating at the highest possible level,
assuming the weight she carried
was just the weight everyone carried.

Sometimes we don't know we've been surviving
until someone shows us the data.

KATHLEEN M.

Only 2.5 Percent

LISA S.

Before I Knew It, the Question Was Out of My Mouth

She was forty-five years old – the same age her father was when he died – when a family member made an offhand comment that started a chain reaction she hadn't been prepared for. She had spent thirty-five years believing her father died of a heart attack. The next time she was with her mother, she asked if he had been depressed. Her mother said yes – something they had never spoken about before. And before she could stop herself, before she even knew she was going to say it, the question was out of her mouth: *did he take his life?* Her mother said yes. And everything she thought she knew about her father, about her grief, about thirty-five years of memory, changed in that single moment.

FOR YOU

Lisa said the truth contaminated everything at first –
and then her husband reminded her
that every laugh, every walk, every real moment with her
father
had still been real.

The truth changed the story.

It didn't change what actually happened between them.

Whatever truth you are holding back from yourself,
or that someone is holding back from you:
it will change things when it lands.

It may also leave the real things intact.

LISA S.

Before I Knew It, the Question
Was Out of My Mouth

MARTHA J.

A Classmate Stands Up

She was a college freshman, standing at the front of the room with her index cards, giving an oral report on Frantz Fanon. She was shaking. Partway through, a classmate stood up and told the room she had no right to be there. Not a classroom disagreement. A declaration. She finished the report. She walked back to her dorm room. And she put on the armor she would wear for decades.

FOR YOU

Her classmate's words didn't diminish her.
They steeled her.

But there is a cost to armor, even necessary armor –
it keeps things out that you might have wanted in.

The sentence someone says to take something from you
can end up shaping just as much of your life
as the sentences that gave.

What have you been carrying
since someone told you that you didn't belong?

MARTHA J.

A Classmate Stands Up

section 6

WHEN LOVE IS THE REASON

Grief is love with nowhere to go.

I've heard that said more than once, and I think it's true –
but I'd add that love with nowhere to go doesn't stay still.
It finds a shape.

It becomes a song you sing in the dark,
a question you ask thirty years too late on a plane,
a poem, a page,
a door you walk toward even though you are terrified of
what's on the other side.

The people in this section were all moved by someone they
couldn't stop loving.

A brother. A mother. A father who died before they could
become close. A dog.

The love didn't go anywhere when the person did.

It just had to find somewhere new to land.

JACLYN L.

The Night Her Sister's House Felt Different

She had overdosed at nineteen. Her sister and brother-in-law came to the ER and asked if she wanted to move in with them. She did – and kept doing the things she had always done, drinking and using drugs, bringing it all into their home. They never judged her. They never threw her out. They just kept loving her, the same way, with everything she carried. She had never seen anything like it. She started asking why. The answer led her somewhere she had never expected to go.

FOR YOU

Jaclyn said rock bottom didn't change her.

What changed her was being loved without condition
while she was still in it –
loved in a way that didn't ask her to be different first.

If you are waiting to be worthy of love before you accept it,
Jaclyn's story is for you.

The love that changed her was given before she earned it.

That's the whole point.

JACLYN L.

The Night Her Sister's House Felt Different

CLAUDIA B.

She Moved Her Car First

She had just had her first cancer surgery. She still had stitches in her neck. She was asleep, recovering, when she woke up for no particular reason and looked out the window to see someone sitting in her little convertible in the driveway. Later, her husband had his car in the shop. She went downstairs, told the nanny she'd be right back, got the family car, and drove to his office – an apartment they used for work. It was raining. She knew before she got there. She parked her convertible in a different lot so he wouldn't see it. Then she walked back through the rain, used her key, and walked through the door. She said she needed to see it because she couldn't believe it. She said: *why would someone do this to me? I was a good wife. I was a good mother.*

FOR YOU

Claudia said betrayal has been part of her life more times than
she can count,
and she keeps asking what lesson she still needs to learn.

But she walked through that door
with stitches in her neck,
in the rain,
on the night after surgery,
because she loved her life
and couldn't believe what was happening to it.

That is not weakness.

That is someone who cared enough to need to know the
truth,
even when the truth was going to cost her everything.

CLAUDIA B.

She Moved Her Car First

SUSAN L.

My Brother Shouldn't Be Home on a Thursday

She was in sixth grade. That morning, she had told her mother she hated her. She came home from school to find her brother standing in the house in the middle of the day, which was wrong – he shouldn't have been home on a Thursday. He looked at her and said: *go pack your bags. Mom's in a coma.* Three days later, their mother died of a botched plastic surgery by a San Francisco doctor who had numerous complaints against him. Susan had said I hate you that morning and never got to take it back.

FOR YOU

Susan spent years carrying that morning –
the words she said,
the brother who shouldn't have been home,
the three days that followed.

What she eventually made from it
was a memoir, a one-woman show,
a way of speaking to her mother in public
that she couldn't do in private.

Grief doesn't just take.

Sometimes it makes us into people
we couldn't have become any other way.

That's not a comfort.

It's just true.

SUSAN L.

My Brother Shouldn't Be Home on a Thursday

LAUREL W.

Daddy's Girl

In the fall of 2017, a film crew came to her Nashville apartment to document a songwriting session. She and her partner wrote a song about her father that day – called her dad several times during the process, asking him to tell her stories from when they were young. Her sister heard the finished song. Their dad hadn't yet. A few months later, on January 5, 2018, her sister died in a car accident. She was two and a half years younger than Laurel. Her only sibling. Then, within that same year, her father died too. The last song her sister ever heard about their dad was a song Laurel had written for him. Laurel didn't know, when she made those phone calls, what that song would become.

FOR YOU

Laurel said she had written her very first song at ten years old
because her great-grandmother had died
and she needed somewhere to put the feeling.

She didn't know then
that she was learning the only language
that would carry her through the worst years of her life.

Whatever you create –
whatever form you've found for putting the feeling
somewhere –
it is practicing for something.

You don't know yet what it's practicing for.

But it's practicing.

LAUREL W.

Daddy's Girl

CYRA D.

The Choice She Made When She Was Sixteen

She was sixteen when her brother died by suicide. She was the one who found him. For years, she carried the weight of that day – the guilt, the questions, the silence around what happened. She didn't have language for it. She found poetry instead. The page became the place where she could put it all down, name it, look at it without being consumed by it. The writing didn't take the grief away. It gave it somewhere to live that wasn't just inside her.

The Choice She Made When She Was Sixteen

FOR YOU

Cyra's story is about what we do
when love doesn't have anywhere to go.

When the person is gone
and the feeling remains
and there's no container for it.

She built one out of words.

You don't have to write poetry.
But whatever you are carrying that has no container –
it might be worth asking what form it could take.

The love doesn't disappear when the person does.

It needs somewhere to go.

CYRA D.

The Choice She Made When She Was Sixteen

MATT F.

Brokedown Palace

His father had been emotionally distant and then was gone – died of cancer at 48 when Matt was in college, before they could ever become close in the way Matt had always hoped they would. Years later, the first night home with his newborn son, nothing was working – the baby screaming, the dog barking, everything wrong. He didn't know what to do. So he started singing. Not a lullaby. A Grateful Dead song. Brokedown Palace. He said it came out of him like a breath – like he gave it no thought at all. He sang it to his son nearly every night for fourteen years.

FOR YOU

Matt said that night was when he started doing fatherhood
differently –
not following the pattern he'd been given
but staking a quiet claim to something new.

You don't have to name what you're changing in order to
change it.

Sometimes you just start singing a Grateful Dead song in the
dark,
and it turns out that's the beginning of everything.

MATT F.

Brokedown Palace

JACKIE F.

The Morning She Left for the Hospital

Her grandmother – her very best friend – died two days before her daughter was born. Her mother couldn't come; she was in Pennsylvania caring for Jackie's grandfather, who had dementia. Her marriage was dissolving. She had spent her whole pregnancy realizing the man she was with could not be what she needed. On the morning of her induction, she walked out the front door of her house. It was December. It was icy. She slipped down the stairs and landed on the concrete. She got up. She went to the hospital alone – ten hours of labor, an emergency C-section, her daughter's heart rate dropping, meconium in the fluid, doctors moving fast. Her husband stood in the far corner of the operating room. The anesthesiologist was the one beside her head. She thought about her grandmother. She thought about her mother. She thought: *I don't know if I'm going to live.* And she felt completely alone.

FOR YOU

Jackie said she had done all the things on the checklist –
college, engagement, house, baby –
and found out that the checklist doesn't guarantee the life.

She was alone in a cold operating room,
having slipped on ice that morning,
with a marriage that was already over.

What came next –
her daughter, her survival, the life she built after –
started in that room.

Not because it was beautiful.

Because she got through it anyway.

JACKIE F.

The Morning She Left
for the Hospital

BRIANNA L.

All This Love and Nowhere to Put It

Molly had been hers since she was fourteen – through every hard year of adolescence, through college, through getting engaged and planning a wedding. By the time the cancer came, Molly was fifteen and had been with Brianna through more of her life than almost anyone. In January, she couldn't walk. The family gathered in the living room and agreed: *tomorrow they would call the vet.* But Molly didn't wait for tomorrow. At 1:30 in the morning, she took her last breath, and Brianna was there. In the weeks after, Brianna said she had all this love to give and nowhere to put it. She didn't know who she was anymore.

FOR YOU

Brianna became a therapist
and got certified in grief
and started helping people who had lost pets –
because she couldn't find anyone who understood what she
was going through
and she decided to become that person for others.

The love that had nowhere to go
found somewhere to go.

That's what love does when you let it.

It doesn't disappear.

It redirects.

BRIANNA L.

All This Love and
Nowhere to Put It

KRISTINA A.

The Stranger's Question

Her brother had told the family for a year and a half that he was going to die young, that it had something to do with a green car. He was thirteen when a green car struck him while he was riding his bike. He lived two hours. Kristina was seventeen. What followed were years of addiction, silence, and grief that had no language and no container. Thirty-five years later, she read a small piece she had written at a writing retreat to a stranger on an airplane. He was an English professor. He listened. And then he asked one question: *who else knew your brother?*

FOR YOU

Kristina had been carrying him for thirty-five years
without knowing she was allowed to put him down
and look at him.

It took one question from a stranger on a plane
to give her permission to go find the people who
remembered her brother.

You probably have something you've been carrying
that was never given its proper name.

It doesn't expire.

It's still there,
waiting for someone to ask the right question.

Sometimes that person is a stranger.

Sometimes it's you.

KRISTINA A.

The Stranger's Question

BARB H.

Her Legs Were Completely Still

She had left for Amsterdam the last week of April 2016. Her thirteen-year-old daughter was furious that she was going. Barb made her say goodbye before she left – told her: *if something happened to me on this trip and you never said goodbye, you would feel horrible for the rest of your life.* They hugged. They talked. Barb left. Her daughter got sick while she was gone. Barb came home to find her in the ER. Sixteen hours of pushing for a CAT scan that no one would order. Then at one in the morning, Barb was holding her daughter's hand when she noticed her legs had gone completely still. She looked up at her daughter's face and watched it turn gray, then blue, then yellow. A brain tumor had ruptured. Her daughter was thirteen years old.

FOR YOU

Barb said she'd been a disaster that year –
drinking, an injury she couldn't work through,
a relationship that had a hold on her,
a marriage living apart.

She carried tremendous guilt afterward.

And then she said:
looking back, even if she had been spot on,
what was missed likely wouldn't have changed.

The guilt of a parent is one of the most unfair weights in the
world.

You were doing what you were doing.

You did not know.

That is not the same as not caring.

BARB H.

Her Legs Were
Completely Still

NADIA C.

I'm Done

She grew up Jehovah's Witness on the island of Sardinia. She knew the rules: if you left, the congregation was no longer allowed to speak to you. That included family. She had been pulling away quietly – not answering the door when they came to check on her, not going to meetings – until one day her mother called and asked what was going on. And Nadia exploded. She told her everything. And then she said the thing she had been building toward for years: *if you don't want to speak to me, I understand. That's the rule. I don't care. I'm done.* Her mother stayed. Nadia didn't look back.

FOR YOU

Nadia said the lie she lived for years –
the performance of belonging to
something she didn't believe –
was not cowardice.

It was survival.

Leaving a closed community means risking everything:
family, identity,
every relationship you were raised inside.

The explosion on the phone wasn't anger.
It was the sound of someone finally telling the truth at full
volume.

Whatever you have been quietly pulling away from –
the conversation you've been building toward
is probably already overdue.

NADIA C.

I'm Done

REBE H.

The Plane Home From Cuba

She was nineteen when her mother was dying in a hospital bed, and she couldn't bring herself to look at her. She stood in the doorway and looked at the floor. She never looked. Her mother died, and she carried that – not just the loss but the looking away – for thirty years. Then she was on a plane home from Cuba, alone with her thoughts, and the memory came back. She replayed it. She looked this time. In her mind, she crossed the room, sat beside her mother, and asked the question she had never asked: *are you scared, Mom?* The tears she had been holding for three decades finally came.

FOR YOU

Rebe said she couldn't look at her mother at nineteen
because she was nineteen.

She wasn't ready.
She wasn't equipped.
None of us are, at nineteen,
for what life sometimes asks of us.

The gift of the plane home from Cuba
is that we can go back.

Not to change it – we can't change it.

But to finally be present for it.

To give the moment what we couldn't give it then.

It's never too late to show up
for something that already happened.

REBE H.

The Plane Home
From Cuba

MATHILDE F.

I Need to Live This Life for Him

She was fifteen years old when her best friend died of cancer. They had watched Friends together during his treatments, talking constantly about New York, about America, about the life they were going to have when they got there. He never got there. He died at fifteen. And something in Mathilde shifted in the grief – not into sorrow alone, but into a kind of fuel. She decided she would go. She would live the dreams they had made together. She would carry him there with her. At seventeen, she talked her parents into letting her go to a summer program in New York. She stood in the immigration line at Newark at 2 a.m. and called her parents from a payphone to say she had made it. Her parents were crying on the other end. She didn't know that until months later.

FOR YOU

Mathilde said she still feels it sometimes –
the sense that she needs to live this life for him.

That might sound like a burden.
It isn't.
It's a reason.

If you have lost someone
who had dreams they never got to chase,
you know this feeling.

The question is whether you let it anchor you
or whether you let it move you.

Mathilde let it move her all the way to New York.

MATHILDE F.

I Need to Live
This Life for Him

TANMEET S.

Why Not Us?

She was nine months pregnant, sitting on the porch bench with her husband, when they were told their three-year-old had a fatal degenerative illness. One of them said – and neither can remember who said it first – *why not us?* Not why me. Why not us. Three words that chose grief and responsibility over bitterness, that decided this was theirs to carry together. A new baby was coming. A child was dying. And somehow, between those two things, a question reframed everything.

FOR YOU

You don't have to like what is happening to you
to decide how you will meet it.

Tanmeet and her husband didn't get to choose the diagnosis.
They chose the posture.

That choice –
toward each other,
toward the life in front of them
rather than the one they had planned –
is available to all of us in any hardship.

It doesn't make the hardship smaller.

It makes you larger than it.

TANMEET S.

Why Not Us?

SALLY M.

Four of Them
Got in a Canoe

It was January 2016. Her son was twenty-one years old, bright and magnetic and beautifully wild. He was up north with friends when four of them decided to get into a canoe on a frozen lake. None of them survived that decision. Sally found out the way you find out in those moments – a phone call that ended everything. He was gone. The life she had been living, the one where he was in it, was over. What followed was years of grief so total she could barely see. It took seven years, she said, to feel like herself again. A different and better version of herself.

FOR YOU

Sally said she knew, going in,
that this kind of loss has a high rate of ending marriages.

She and her husband chose to face it together anyway,
giving each other room to grieve differently,
at different paces, in different ways.

She said love is the only thing that matters.

She means it the way people mean things
after they have paid everything to learn them.

Keep your heart wide open
even when you want to protect it.

That was her message.
She earned the right to say it.

SALLY M.

Four of Them
Got in a Canoe

KATHLEEN Q.

The Recliners

Her husband had pancreatic cancer. Five months, maybe less. She was doing everything right – the spreadsheets, the communication, the CaringBridge page, the daily drives to the park to watch the cellist and hold his hand. She had ordered special recliners from a store in Portland because the Costco ones weren't good enough for him, and they kept getting delayed. She got off the phone with the store. She texted her best friend: *get the Costco ones, I'm done.* She looked at her husband sitting in his chair with the music on, his feet tapping, and she said: *I'm going to the grocery store.* She walked out and slammed it. She screamed at a stranger on the phone. She was furious about recliners. She knew it wasn't about the recliners.

FOR YOU

On their first date, her husband had looked at her over coffee
at Christmas and asked: *what do you miss most about your
mom at the holidays?*

She married that man.
She spent 27 years with that man.

The recliner was not a breakdown.
It was the one crack in five months of nearly perfect love
in the face of the impossible.

If you are holding everything together for someone you love
and you break once over something ridiculous –
a recliner, a parking spot, a wrong takeout order –
that is not a failure.

That is what five months of grace costs.

KATHLEEN Q.

The Recliners

LORI K.

I Brought Him Here

She and her husband had moved to Tennessee from the Washington area, and a year later, she called her son. He was unhappy at work, she said. Come down, manage the rental properties, get your real estate license. He thought about it. He said yes. He moved. He was thirty-three years old, his business beginning to pick up, his own house, his own dog. Lived just down the road. And then he was gone – in an accident five minutes from their home. The proximity of it never left her. She had asked him to come. She had brought him there.

FOR YOU

Lori said she had been living a pretty normal life before this –
no real trauma, no preparation for loss like this.

What she did with it was write.
A novel. A blog.

A way of giving language to grief that had no container.

The love that brought him to Tennessee
became the love that kept going after he was gone.

Sometimes the thing that costs us most
is also the thing that opens us to our truest purpose.

That's not a comfort.
It's just what happened.

LORI K.

I Brought Him Here

section 7

THE DOOR YOU DIDN'T KNOW WAS THERE

Some shifts don't happen to you and don't come from a decision.

They arrive the way light comes through a crack – unexpected, impossible to predict, impossible to manufacture.

You were not looking for this.
You could not have planned for this.
And yet here it is, and here you are,
and something has opened that you didn't know was closed.

I find these stories the hardest to explain and the easiest to feel. They resist the language of cause and effect.
A shark. A hard seltzer in a ski resort parking lot.
A temple in a city built for the dead.
A stranger diving toward you in dark water.

You can't engineer the door.
You can only be present enough to
walk through it when it appears.

NISHA A.

Arrested in Burma

She had been an activist since college – getting arrested for causes, protesting whatever needed protesting. At the circus, locked by the neck to other activists in the center ring, she saw the families filing in and had a thought she hadn't had before: this isn't right. Not the cause. The tactic. She started to understand something about strategy and empathy that she couldn't have articulated yet. Two years later, she was in Burma on what was supposed to be an educational trip to the Thai-Burma border, until a woman handed her a business-card-sized leaflet and a plan. Nisha hid the leaflet in the sole of her shoe and handed it out for five minutes on the anniversary of a massacre. She was arrested. All eighteen of them were. She had been sentenced to five years of hard labor in a military dictatorship before international pressure got her out. It changed everything about how she understood the world.

FOR YOU

Nisha said what the circus taught her
was that being morally right isn't enough.
You also have to be strategic.
You have to understand who else is in the room
and what they need.

That's not a compromise –
it's how things actually change.

Whatever it is you're trying to do or fix or build,
it's worth asking not just if you're right,
but whether the way you're doing it
is actually working.

NISHA A.

Arrested in Burma

EMILY H.

The Hard Seltzer
at Winter Park

She had been drinking since she was thirteen. She didn't think of herself as an alcoholic – her life looked fine from the outside, and she had spent years measuring herself against people who had it worse. After Dry January, she had a few drinks in February, and then one afternoon, she was skiing at Winter Park with friends and cracked a hard seltzer in the parking lot. She drank half of it. And suddenly she felt like she didn't have control of her limbs. She hated the feeling. She looked at herself in the dropdown mirror of her car and told herself: *this is the last drink I want to have.* She didn't even finish it. She has not had one since.

FOR YOU

Emily said she did so many worse things while drinking before
that moment –
and it was this tiny, ordinary can of seltzer
that was finally the one.

She didn't plan it.
She didn't have a big dramatic rock bottom.
She just looked in a mirror and knew.

Sometimes, the moment that changes your life
is not the biggest thing that ever happened to you.

It's just the first one you were finally ready to hear.

EMILY H.

The Hard Seltzer
at Winter Park

TIM T.

His Friend's Eyes

He was a Special Forces operator who had built his whole life around performing at the highest level and trusting no one to carry his weight. Then he was attacked by a shark off Sydney, his leg in its mouth, bleeding in the water. He looked up and saw his friend diving toward him. And what he felt was not relief exactly – it was something else. A curtain of stress fell from his body, from his head to his feet, in a single instant. He felt pure trust. He had never felt it before. He said it was the moment that cracked open a life that had only ever looked inward.

FOR YOU

Tim spent years believing that needing other people was a
weakness.

It took a shark and a friend
diving toward him in the water
to show him that trust is not vulnerability –
it's the thing that keeps you alive.

Most of us will never be in the water with a shark.

But most of us have been somewhere
we couldn't get out of alone,
waiting to see if someone would dive in.

The question is whether we let ourselves feel it when they do.

TIM T.

His Friend's Eyes

JASMIN F.

I Heard Them Talking About Me

She grew up between Saudi Arabia and Italy, code-switching between two worlds, hiding her Italian heart inside the restrictions of a country that wanted to silence her. She had always known the moment was coming – the moment she got her period, she would officially become a woman, and everything that came with that would close around her. One afternoon, she overheard her mother and a friend asking whether she had become a young lady yet. Her mother said not yet. That was the shift. She understood in that moment exactly what they were waiting for. She got her period a few months later and hid it for an entire year. Her younger sister got hers first, before Jasmin disclosed her own. That hidden year was the beginning of the rest of her life.

FOR YOU

Jasmin said she believed she deserved better –
not in a materialistic way,
but on a spiritual level.

She felt called to maximize the life she had been given.

Most of us have a version of that knowing inside us.

The question is whether we trust it enough to protect it –
even for a year – until we can find a way to live it.

JASMIN F.

I Heard Them
Talking About Me

ALLISON S.

The Temple at Varanasi

After a medical freefall that had left her feeling already dead – no joy, no presence, no work, no way forward – she traveled alone to India and made her way to the temple of the goddess Kali in Varanasi, the city where the Hindu dead are placed into the Ganges. She wore a sari of black and red. She knelt before the goddess. And then she slipped into what she calls sacred time – she lost her ego, she lost track of how long she was there, and everything that had been holding her in the land of the dead burned away. She walked out of the temple weeping, putting herself back together piece by piece.

FOR YOU

Allison said she had to do something that terrified her
and broke every familiar pattern –
because if she kept doing the comfortable thing
she would never break through.

Whatever you've been circling that scares you –
the thing you keep finding reasons not to try –
it might be the door.

You don't have to go to India.

But you might have to go somewhere you've never been
before.

ALLISON S.

The Temple at Varanasi

SUZANNE A.

She Smashed It on the Hearth

Her husband had died by suicide. A psychologist, a researcher, a woman who had spent her career studying how people grow – and she was standing at the edge of something she had no framework for. In the early days of grief, she gathered with friends, and someone began a shamanic rattling. At the peak moment, Suzanne picked up one of her husband's rare ceramic vessels – a beautiful thing he had collected – and smashed it on the stone hearth. It broke into pieces. The room went silent. And something in her body understood what her mind was still trying to accept: there was no going back. There was no there there anymore. This was her life now.

FOR YOU

Suzanne said the moment she could get that understanding
into her body –
not just her mind –
was the moment she could begin.

Grief lives in the intellect for a long time
before it lands somewhere deeper.

The smashing of the vessel was a message to herself
that she meant it,
that she accepted it,
that she was going to try to live fully anyway.

What does it look like for you to get your grief into your body?

Sometimes it takes something physical
to make the abstract real.

SUZANNE A.

She Smashed It
on the Hearth

LEAH F.

It Slipped Out of My Back Pocket

She had been a psychotherapist for thirty-five years – sitting in a chair, having intimate conversations with people, holding their stories. She was good at it. And then someone died, and it did what deaths do: it made her ask the question. *When it's my turn, what am I really going to regret not having done?* And the answer came immediately. There was a dream she had been carrying for the better part of forty years. She had kept it in her back pocket – it was always there, but that wasn't where her focus was. In the moment after the question, it slipped out and was right in her face. She closed her practice. She took a solo sabbatical. She was in her sixties. She went to the Amazon jungle.

FOR YOU

Leah said the dream had been in her back pocket for forty
years.

Not forgotten. Just waiting.

The death didn't create the dream –
it just finally made the dream too loud to keep filing away.

If you have something in your back pocket
that you keep meaning to get to,
it is worth asking how long you are going to keep it there.

The question isn't whether the dream is still alive.

It clearly is.

The question is: what are you waiting for?

LEAH F.

It Slipped Out of
My Back Pocket

LEVI K.

The Tap on the Shoulder

He was deep in a crystal meth addiction, at the back of a club, fully engaged in using, when he felt a tap on his shoulder. A young man stood there, wide-eyed, looking for his friend. He said: *are you Levi?* He said yes. The young man said: *I listened to your album the whole way here and it's making such a difference as I'm trying to understand coming out.* Levi sat there and tried to take the moment in. He was high, and the moment was gone almost as quickly as it arrived. But it stayed. He said those moments kept becoming more common – being caught between the life he was hiding and the life he was trying to create. The tap on the shoulder was the first crack in the wall.

FOR YOU

Levi said the crack came before the rock bottom,
before the doctor's visit that finally
made stopping non-negotiable.

It came from a stranger in the back of a club
who had no idea what he was interrupting.

Most of us have had a version of that tap –
a moment where something outside us
reflected back something we weren't ready to see.

The question isn't whether the tap comes.

The question is whether we let it land.

LEVI K.

The Tap on the Shoulder

ELEN S.

The Man on the Stage

She was a software engineer and a dancer – two full lives, running in parallel. Then one January morning, she woke up and couldn't move her shoulder. Then the other shoulder. Then a hip, then a knee that swelled to the size she couldn't believe. The rheumatoid arthritis took both lives from her overnight. She got very depressed. She said if she couldn't dance, she didn't know if she wanted to go on. Her cats lay on her and kept her there. Eventually, friends took her to a lecture. She didn't know what it was about. A large man was on the stage with a beautiful voice, and she said that after five minutes, he could have been reading the phone directory, and she would have been riveted. Something he said went into her in a way she couldn't explain. She staggered up to the stage afterward and said she wanted to sign on. It turned out to be transpersonal psychology – the field she would spend the rest of her life practicing.

FOR YOU

Elen said without the rheumatoid arthritis,
she wouldn't be where she is now.

She didn't start there.

She started in the depression and the not wanting to go on.

The disease didn't give her the new life –
she chose the new life, in the ruins of the old one.

What has been taken from you
that you haven't yet allowed to become a door?

ELEN S.

The Man on the Stage

PAMELA T.

The Water Bottle

She had just left her second abusive marriage. She thought this time things would finally be okay. Instead, the childhood trauma she had been outrunning for years came crashing down all at once – nightmares, night terrors, depression, the feeling of sinking deeper every day with no way to stop it. She was thinking about suicide. A friend mentioned California. Two weeks later, she had sold everything, bought a one-way bus ticket, and gotten on a three-day ride across the country with no plan and no return. She was numb. She was just moving. And then the person who sat down next to her on the bus pulled out a water bottle. It wasn't filled with water.

FOR YOU

Pamela said she got on that bus as a last-ditch effort.

She didn't know it was a door.
She just knew she had to move or she was going to stop.

Sometimes the bravest thing a person does
is buy a ticket to somewhere and get on.

You don't have to know where you're going.
You just have to go.

The door you didn't know was there
might be on a three-day bus ride
with a stranger who also needed a way out.

PAMELA T.

The Water Bottle

CHRIS G.

Me and Him on a Concrete Block

He had grown up searching for who he was in all the wrong places, finding the party scene because at least it was something. October 13, 2002. Downtown Nashville. Broadway was a ghost town on a Sunday night – not the Nashville anyone knows today. He stood on a concrete block and had an internal conversation with God. He said: *I'm done. I'm tired, I'm broken, I'm empty, I'm hurting. I can't do this anymore. If you are who you say you are, I'm going to give you my life.* He said it. And radically, he said, his life changed forever. It wasn't in a service. It wasn't in a crowd. It was just him and that concrete block on an empty street.

FOR YOU

Chris has a picture on his wall of that exact spot.

The most important moment of his life
happened with no audience, no ceremony, and no
announcement.

Just a person at the end of themselves
on an empty street
saying the only honest thing left to say.

You don't need a crowd for the moment that changes
everything.

Sometimes it just needs you
and the truth about where you are.

CHRIS G.

Me and Him
on a Concrete Block

ASH P.

I Became Ripples

He was dying. Not metaphorically – clinically, in the way that bodies sometimes go. And what he felt was not what he expected. He became ripples. That's the only way he could describe it: his consciousness expanding outward into the universe with no edges, no separation, just ripples going and going and going. He had a thought that surprised him: *oh, I didn't think dying would be like this.* He felt curious. And then, from somewhere inside that expanding dissolution, he heard himself say: *I want to stay.* That was the moment. Not the dying. The wanting to stay.

FOR YOU

Ash had spent years before that moment living in survival
mode –
stacking accomplishments,
trying to hold everything together,
looking inward and never outward.

The expansion he felt in those last moments
wasn't something the living version of him
had ever allowed himself.

He had to almost not come back
to learn that he wanted to.

Most of us won't get that particular lesson that way.

But the question underneath it
is one we can ask without dying:
what would you want to stay for?

Whatever your answer is,
it's worth living toward now.

ASH P.

I Became Ripples

MARIE A.

The Rug Was Pulled Right Underneath My Feet

She was getting the kids sorted when the coroner's office called. Her husband had died suddenly while away on a business trip. It pulled the rug right out from underneath her feet – her own words – and she slipped into a world that felt surreal, where she had come to a standstill, and everything around her kept spinning. The life they had built together, intentionally, from the ground up, from a soul level she would only later understand, had just split into before and after. What followed wasn't only grief. Years before he died, they had made a promise to each other about how they wanted to live. She chose to keep it – not instead of the pain, but alongside it. Not because it was easy. Because it was what they had already decided together.

FOR YOU

Marie said she lived happiness –
you could feel it even in the hard parts of the story.

That wasn't denial.
That was a decision made long before she needed it.

She and her husband had chosen how they wanted to live
before either of them knew what was coming.

After he died, that choice became the thing that carried her.

Some of us won't have that promise already in place.
But the question underneath her story
is one worth sitting with now,
before anything pulls the rug out:
what have you already decided
about how you want to live?

Because that decision is available to you right now.

Make it.

MARIE A.

The Rug Was Pulled Right
Underneath My Feet

DAN M.

Mind the Gap

He was on the tube in London, living the fast life – global travel, a career that moved, Friday night pints – when the lights went out. Not the train lights. His. He lost his vision on the platform, suddenly and completely. He was blind. Within days, he was in emergency brain surgery. He woke up from a coma to find that the life he had been running at full speed was not available anymore. The recovery was long, with setbacks that kept arriving. A malpractice lawsuit, an eye surgery that backfired and took away more than it fixed. He keeps going anyway. He calls it being better than yesterday.

FOR YOU

Dan said he gets sick of telling the story –
that the fun part for him is what comes after,
the daily hacks for getting back to yourself.

But the story is the thing
that makes the hacks mean something.
You don't get to skip past the tube platform
and the dark and the coma
and arrive at the better version.

You go through it.

And if you can find one thing to be better at today
than you were yesterday,
you can build a life out of that.

He did.

DAN M.

Mind the Gap

DANIEL B.

There Are No Dragons at Dulles

He was sitting in an airline lounge at Dulles Airport. Ivy League degrees. A law career. A fast track to the State Department. Everything checked. Then he started hearing things. Then he started seeing things. A large dragon flying around the roof of the lounge. He knew airline lounges didn't have dragons. He knew he was in trouble. He had not slept in days. He was taken to a psychiatric hospital, where he collapsed on the floor in front of a woman and a loaf of bread. The smart kid who had won all the awards without trying was now a patient in a room that had no space for the life he had built.

FOR YOU

Dan said he left the armor behind after that.

Not all at once –
it took years, and a career reinvention into fine jewelry and
legacy storytelling,
and learning to walk into hard rooms without his defenses on.

But he said something that stays:
weeping for wonder, even here.
Not weeping for pain or for what was lost.

For wonder.

That it's still possible to be amazed by being alive,
even after the dragon and the floor and the hospital.

Especially then.

DANIEL B.

There Are No Dragons
at Dulles

ISABELLE D.

Three Days on the Floor in Hawaii

Her family had gone to dinner. She stayed behind in the hotel room, too much pain to go. She lay on the floor the way she always did when it was bad – back flat, legs up on the chair at ninety degrees, the only position that helped. She had been living like this for years. A decade of chronic pain, an identity she'd lost, a body she no longer recognized, a marriage and a motherhood she felt she was failing at all at once. That night, she cried harder than she ever had. And she said the first real prayer of her life. She didn't know who she was praying to. She said: *I don't know how to do this. I don't know where else to go. Help me.* And then her body started shaking. Her torso lifted off the wooden floor, vibrating from her tailbone, her whole frame unwinding. She didn't know what was happening. She felt completely at peace. It went on for three days and three nights. Every time she had to crawl to the bathroom, it would stop. On her way back, it would start again. She said she knew, even in those three days, that it was right. That was the turning point.

FOR YOU

Isabelle had spent a decade running into walls –
the walls of her pain,
her identity,
her resistance to the person she was becoming.

She was stubborn about surrendering, she says,
in a way that most people aren't.

It took three days on a hotel floor in Hawaii
for something to finally move through her
that her mind couldn't manage alone.

You don't have to go that far.

But if you've been running into the same wall,
it might be worth asking
what you've never been willing to put down.

ISABELLE D.

Three Days on the
Floor in Hawaii

ERIN B.

Whatever is in the Highest

She had found what she thought was the life she had always wanted – a stable home, a partner she loved, his son, a sense of family she hadn't had in her adult life. Then one night her partner had a heart attack. She called 911. The paramedics came and went to work. She stepped back behind the couch. And standing there, watching, she heard herself say words she hadn't planned: *whatever is in the highest, whatever is in the highest.* She was not a praying person. She didn't know why she said it. But she said it. And she knew, even as she said it, that she was letting go – not because she wanted to, but because some part of her already understood that this was not hers to hold.

FOR YOU

Erin said she was a type A, hyper-achieving, plan-everything person.

The surrender didn't come from her nature.
It came from somewhere underneath her nature,
something that knew what she wasn't ready to know.

Most of us have a version of that underneath –
something that understands things before our mind does.

It speaks in moments we would never have chosen.

The question is whether we can hear it when it does.

ERIN B.

Whatever is in the Highest

section 8

THE SECRET YOU CARRIED

This is the quietest section of the book.

It holds the things
that were never supposed to be said out loud –
the secrets kept from people,
the silences imposed on children,
the burdens that lived underground for years
because there was no other place for them.

These are not my stories to tell completely.
I am only the witness.
What I can say is this:
every person in this section
took a step toward putting the thing down.

Not forgetting it.
Not making it disappear.
Just beginning to stop carrying it alone.
Some of them are still in that process.
That is also allowed.

DONNA K.

The Made Bed

She came home to get ready for a date. She was putting on her blouse, getting herself together for the evening, when something pulled her toward the bedroom. She opened the door. The bed was made. One thing her husband never did – not once, not ever – was make the bed. She stood there looking at it. She knew before she opened the closet. The made bed was the moment. The thing he had done in his last hours was make the bed so no one would walk in on a messy room. She understood what that meant before her mind had words for it.

FOR YOU

Donna didn't collapse in the doorway.
She moved. She called.
She kept going because there were children
and because there was no other option
and because something in her had already decided,
in that moment in front of the made bed,
that she was going to survive this.

She didn't know that yet.
But her body did.

I don't know what it is about the small, mundane details
that break us open in ways the large facts can't.

The made bed did more than any word could.

Sometimes the truth of a thing
lives in the most ordinary object in the room.

DONNA K.

The Made Bed

ALYSE M.

I Need to Tell You Something

She had told her mother when she was fourteen. Her mother didn't believe her. Child Protective Services came to her school unannounced, interviewed her in the middle of religion class, and the story didn't match – because she was scared, because she didn't know they were coming. There were inconsistencies. He walked free. She stayed angry for almost ten years. Then she was in college, and she was in the middle of a hard night, and at 3 a.m., she texted her mother: *I need to tell you something, and you need to understand that I'm telling you the truth.* Her mother divorced him that day.

FOR YOU

Alyse said she eventually came to understand that her mother
was a victim too –
that the abuser's job is to make it impossible for anyone to
know what to believe,
and that her mother had four children
and a life built around this man
and nowhere obvious to go.

Alyse came to show her grace.
That didn't make the ten years of anger wrong.

Both things were true.

The 3 a.m. text was an act of extraordinary courage
from someone who had already been failed once
and was willing to try again anyway.

ALYSE M.

I Need to Tell You Something

WENDY C.

The Truth That Pissed Her Off First

She was seven when her father died, and nobody sat her down to explain it. Nobody said she was allowed to be angry. The world just kept moving, and she moved with it. For sixty-two years, she felt like she didn't quite belong in her family – a quiet question she didn't know she was asking, a sense that something was slightly off that no one would acknowledge. Then a DNA test told her the truth: the man who died when she was seven was not her biological father. Her mother had known the whole time. Her biological father had come to the house while her father was at work. The clock on the wall that she had loved her whole life without knowing why had been a gift from him.

FOR YOU

Wendy said the truth set her free –
and first it pissed her off.

Both things are true at the same time
and both deserve to be named.

If you have been sensing something your whole life
that no one will confirm,
your instincts are not broken.

The thing you've been feeling in the room
that no one will name –
it might be real.

And knowing might be worth the pissed-off part.

WENDY C.

The Truth That
Pissed Her Off First

ERIN S.

The Finger to His Lips

She was nine years old, sleeping over at a friend's house, sleeping bags on the floor of the front room. She woke up on her side with burning pain she had never felt before. Something in her knew to be quiet, knew to pretend she was still sleeping. She fluttered her eyes open and saw her friend's father standing over her. When she couldn't take the pain anymore, she started squirming. He stopped. He stood up and straightened her underwear – awkwardly, wrong. And then he put his finger to his lips. The next morning, he handed her a plate of pancakes and looked her in the eyes, and they both knew. She carried it alone.

FOR YOU

Erin said she didn't even have language

for what had happened

because nobody had talked to her about any of this.

She was nine.

She just knew she was supposed to be quiet

and that it was a secret.

If you are carrying something

that was made a secret before you were old enough

to understand what it was –

the silence was not yours to keep.

It was put on you.

You can put it down.

ERIN S.

The Finger to His Lips

KAILA Y.

I Don't Remember That Night

She was in her early twenties. She went to an apartment. What happened there, she doesn't remember – not then, not now. She pushed it all down, locked it somewhere, and pretended it never happened. She didn't tell a single person. She didn't talk to anyone about it until recently. She kept going as two people: Kaila, the name she put into the world, and Elaine, the name that carried what happened that night. For years, the two didn't have to meet. That was the point.

FOR YOU

Kaila told me that even now, decades later,
she can think about that night
and feel like it happened to someone else.

She said her whole life, and a lot of her therapy,
has been about trying to integrate those two –
the public self
and the one who was there that night.

That split was how she survived it.
It's also what keeps her from being fully in one piece.

If you have a version of yourself
that you stored somewhere to protect the rest of you –
they're still there.

They kept.
And they are not asking you to be ready.

They are just asking you to know they exist.

KAILA Y.

I Don't Remember
That Night

CHRISTINA O.

A Lot of Things Started Clicking

She had been in the relationship for a long time before the night he chased her through the house. She tripped. She broke her collarbone. She didn't go to the ER – she went to a friend whose mother worked there, kept it off the record, kept it quiet. But something shifted in that fall. She said a lot of things started clicking. She looked back and understood for the first time what had been happening to her. She didn't leave that night. She planned. She was working 60 hours a week, and she deliberately dropped down to a minimum-wage job and changed her hours so she would be gone when he was home. She made herself invisible until she could make herself gone. Nobody would know when she was leaving. That was the only way out.

FOR YOU

Christina said she didn't recognize what was happening while
she was inside it.

That is not a failure of intelligence or strength –
it is what these situations are designed to do.

The recognition came through her body before it came
through her mind.

A broken collarbone and a set of things that suddenly clicked.
If something in your body is telling you something
your mind hasn't caught up to yet,
the body is usually right.

It got there first.

Listen to it.

CHRISTINA O.

A Lot of Things
Started Clicking

SUZANNE R.

The Light That Found Her

She was five years old. It happened on the living room floor. Her family was in the room. She screamed. No one came. And then something happened that she has spent the rest of her life trying to understand: she went into what she calls a holy state of consciousness, a dissociative state, and in that state she felt bathed by mercy and grace and love. Held by a force she couldn't name. The abuse went on for years. But that presence stayed. Decades later, when she finally said to her mother – not looking at her, sitting beside her – *is it true?* Her mother said yes and cried. They never spoke of it again. Suzanne said she didn't need anything more than that.

FOR YOU

Suzanne said the thing she had to learn
was that the holiness she felt in that dissociative state
wasn't something separate from her –
it was her.

That it had been inside her all along,
not a rescue from outside
but something native and permanent.

Whatever you have survived,
whatever you had to go somewhere else to get through –
the light that held you then is still there.

It was never external.

It was always you.

SUZANNE R.

The Light That Found Her

DEVIN D.

Not Your Story

Her mother had been killed, and the grief had been going on for years in the way grief goes when there are no tools and no one around who knows how to hold it. She had reached a place where she was considering not going on. She was alone in a bathroom. She started to lean into that idea, to let herself move toward it, when she heard the loudest no she had ever heard in her life – a voice right there, right next to her, screaming the word. She was alone. She talked back to it. The voice said: *this is not your story. This is not how your story ends. Your story is meant to be shared with other people.* She said okay. She kept going.

FOR YOU

Devin said she didn't know what that voice was.

She still doesn't, not completely.
What she knows is that it was louder than everything else in
the room.

Some of us will recognize this –
the moment when something inside us,
something we can't fully name,
said no before we could.
You don't have to explain what it was.

You just have to keep being glad it spoke.

DEVIN D.

Not Your Story

SHIGEKO I.

You Need to Relax

She was a teenager in Japan, newly returned from a summer in California, where she had seen, for the first time, what a loving family looked like. Coming home to her own – cold, distant, emotionally empty – was more than she could reconcile. She became argumentative. She stopped sleeping. She was searching for herself in a household and a culture that had no room for that. One night, her brother, a doctor, came into her room with a syringe. He said she needed to relax, that this would help. She said no. He gave her the shot anyway. Several days later, she woke up in a mental hospital room. She had no idea how she had gotten there, or where she was, or how long she had been under. When she finally got home and asked her mother what she had been hospitalized for, her mother said: *you got the illness of a spoiled, ungrateful, entitled child*. She stopped asking.

FOR YOU

Shigeko said that without that experience
she probably wouldn't be living in America,
and she wouldn't have written her book.

She doesn't say that to make it okay.

She says it because the only thing she found
more powerful than what was done to her
was her own insistence on getting out and living differently.

If you have been told by someone who should have
protected you
that your pain was your own fault –
it wasn't.

The syringe was not a cure.

The diagnosis was not yours to carry.

SHIGEKO I.

You Need to Relax

KAREN D.

The Dog in the Doorway

She was twelve and a half years old. She had been living with what her father did to her and her sisters, and that night she stood over him while he slept with a knife. She was ready. Then her dog Boy walked into the room. He grabbed her arm and led her out of the house, down to the river. She stood at the water. And she heard a voice say: *you are loved*. She believed it. She put the knife down. She walked back.

FOR YOU

Karen said she believed the voice.

She was twelve and a half years old
and had every reason not to believe anything that kind,
and she believed it anyway.

Something in her recognized it as true.

Whatever you are carrying,
however long you have been carrying it,
that voice is still speaking.

The question is whether you can be still enough
to hear it.

KAREN D.

The Dog in the Doorway

STILL LISTENING

I started asking strangers about the pivotal moments of their lives because I was trying to understand my own.

I didn't know that at the time. I thought I was building a podcast. I thought I was curious about other people. Both of those things were true. But underneath them was something I hadn't been willing to name: I was eight years old when life shifted, and I still didn't know what to do with what had happened to me, and I was hoping that if I listened to enough people talk about their own lines in the sand, I might figure it out.

It worked. Slowly, and not in the way I expected, but it worked. What I found out is this: the line in the sand is not the end of the story. It feels like the end. In the moment it happens, it feels like the whole world has narrowed to that single point, and everything after it will only ever be aftermath.

But it isn't. The line is just the line. What you do on the other side of it is still yours to write.

I also found out that grief doesn't finish. It changes shape. It gets quieter, usually, and more familiar, and you learn to carry it differently – not because the weight gets lighter but because you get stronger, or at least more practiced.

The people in this book who went through hard things are not over what happened to them. They are living alongside it. And the people who found something – a calling, a door, a moment of unexpected grace – are still tending to it. Both of those things require the same thing: showing up.

That's actually the whole thing.

I found out that human beings are astoundingly, almost unreasonably resilient. I knew this in theory. Sitting across from two hundred and fifty people and watching them tell you about the moment their life broke open – and then watching their face as they describe what happened after – teaches you something about that resilience that you can't get from a theory. It is real. It is in every single person I've ever spoken to. I believe it is in you.

And I found out that the act of telling your story changes it. Not the facts – the facts stay the same. But something about saying it out loud, being witnessed, having another person sit with you in it – that does something to the story that silence never can. I have watched this happen in real time, over and over. People come in holding something alone, and they leave having held it together with someone else for an hour. That hour matters.

It matters more than I can say.

I am still listening. I will keep asking the question.

What was the moment?
What did it feel like?
What did your life look like on the other side of it?

But I want to ask you something too, now that you've been in these rooms with me.

Where is your line in the sand?

Not for me. Not for anyone else. Just for you, quietly, if you've never let yourself really look at it. The moment everything split. The before and the after. The version of yourself you've been carrying since then, alongside the version you show the world.

You don't have to share it with anyone. But I hope you'll sit with it for a moment. I hope you'll give it the attention it deserves. Because it is part of you, and you are worth understanding.

242

Thank you for being here.

Thank you for listening.

9 781639 011858